Sell Your Business for an Outrageous Price

Sell Your Business for an Outrageous Price

AN INSIDER'S GUIDE TO GETTING MORE THAN
YOU EVER THOUGHT POSSIBLE

Kevin M. Short
with
Kathryn A. Bolinske

AMACOM
AMERICAN MANAGEMENT ASSOCIATION
New York • Atlanta • Brussels • Chicago • Mexico City • San Francisco
Shanghai • Tokyo • Toronto • Washington, D.C.

Bulk discounts available. For details visit:
www.amacombooks.org/go/specialsales
Or contact special sales:
Phone: 800-250-5308
E-mail: specialsls@amanet.org
View all the AMACOM titles at: www.amacombooks.org
American Management Association: www.amanet.org

This publication is designed to provide accurate and authoritative information in regard to the subject matter covered. It is sold with the understanding that the publisher is not engaged in rendering legal, accounting, or other professional service. If legal advice or other expert assistance is required, the services of a competent professional person should be sought.

Library of Congress Cataloging-in-Publication Data

Short, Kevin M.
 Sell your business for an outrageous price : an insider's guide to getting more than you ever thought possible / Kevin M. Short, with Kathryn A. Bolinske.
    pages cm.
 Includes bibliographical references and index.
 ISBN 978-0-8144-3471-0 (alk. paper) — ISBN 0-8144-3471-1 (alk. paper) 1. Sale of business enterprises.
I. Bolinske, Kathryn A. II. Title.
 HD1393.25.S46 2015
 658.1'64—dc23
                                                        2014016982

About AMA
American Management Association (www.amanet.org) is a world leader in talent development, advancing the skills of individuals to drive business success. Our mission is to support the goals of individuals and organizations through a complete range of products and services, including classroom and virtual seminars, webcasts, webinars, podcasts, conferences, corporate and government solutions, business books, and research. AMA's approach to improving performance combines experiential learning—learning through doing—with opportunities for ongoing professional growth at every step of one's career journey.

Printing number

10 9 8 7 6 5 4 3 2 1

To my parents,
Mike and Carolyn Short

Contents

Acknowledgments

First, I thank the many business owners who have trusted me with the sale of their businesses. Without them, this book would not be possible.

Nor could I have written without the support of my high school principal, lifelong mentor, and *una donna Stupenda* Sister Mary Ann Eckhoff, SSND (1930-2009).

I thank my family for their patience and support as I put in the long hours and many miles necessary to build my business.

I am grateful to Paula Reeb, my business partner and right hand in all of my entrepreneurial enterprises, for her support and counsel.

For prodding and writing assistance, I thank my writing partner and friend, Kathryn Bolinske. Without her, this book would not be complete, much less written as well as it is.

Finally, thanks to John Brown, whose friendship and writing inspired me.

Sell Your Business for an Outrageous Price

Introduction

For years, I've been preoccupied by a nagging question: Why do similar companies sell at wildly divergent prices? While I admit that this question does not rank with What is the meaning of life? or What goes on in the teenage brain?, like those questions, it has given me its share of sleepless nights. Unlike those two profound questions, however, my ultimate question is one that I had hope I might one day be able to answer.

When I started my career as an investment adviser, I bought companies as investment vehicles for clients. I would analyze both the current and the potential value of companies using every available financial measure. If, for example, Acme Company and Beta Company were of similar value, they'd sell at roughly equivalent prices. But every once in a while, I'd watch Beta sell for two times the purchase price of Acme. What was going on?

My job as an investment adviser was to find the best return for my clients—a task made easier if I didn't overpay for a company. So my interest in answering the question of why comparable companies sold at varying prices was limited to making sure I wasn't the one paying the Outrageous Price.

Note: Throughout this book, I define *Outrageous Price* as one that is at least two times the EBITDA (earnings before interest, taxes, depreciation, and amortization) multiple of an average company in its industry.

In 1991, I entered the world I occupy now: investment banking in the midmarket. I represented then, and do today, owners who want to sell their companies valued between $10 million and $150 million.

I chose investment banking as a career for reasons both practical and emotional. After I sold my investment advisory company to my employees, I spent several years running a number of companies I had purchased. While I loved the challenge of finding new sales outlets, increasing customer loyalty, and launching new product lines, I did not enjoy the too many hours I spent managing personnel. When the opportunity arose to sell my company (at a price that gave my family financial security), I debated. Sell, but then what would I do? Or stay, grow the business, and hope conditions would be favorable at a later date when I was ready to sell? After consulting my family and my advisers, I took the leap and sold.

For six months after closing, I spent time with my wife and our children, whom I'd heard about but hadn't really met. I thought about what I wanted to do next and considered everything from full-time charity work to creating an incubator for business start-ups. I was acutely aware of the tremendous opportunity I enjoyed to choreograph the next step in my life, so I spent hours reading every book about decision making that I could get my hands on. I wanted to make sure I made the best possible decision as I took my next step, but I also wanted to erect a practical framework to support the intuitive way I'd been making decisions throughout my life.

When a friend proposed over lunch one day that I join as a partner in her investment banking firm, I recognized that I had experience in both buying and selling companies as well as the financial analysis skills to do the work. I knew that I could bring valuable insights into how owners think because I'd been an owner and would be again.

It wasn't much of a surprise when I began to observe the same phenomenon as an investment banker that I had as an investment adviser: Seemingly similar companies were selling at very different prices. Again, I wondered why that occurred and sought the data that might yield an answer. The companies I'm talking about here, however, are privately held, so there are no public statistics to dissect—only veiled hints from former owners who hold their cards close to their vests or incredibly tall tales from owners boasting over cocktails.

For me as an investment banker, my question became less academic and more practical, as I had a vested interest in making sure that my seller clients got as much money for their companies as possible. I quickly understood that, as it does in all transactions, leverage played a key role. If the seller had leverage, the sale price went up. If the buyer had it, the sale price was held in check. My ultimate question then evolved into: How can I increase my clients' leverage? Or more intriguing still: Can I create leverage for sellers?

The search for this answer led me to return to the books. I found that Harvard professor Michael E. Porter's theory of competitive advantage gave me a springboard for answering my ultimate question, as his life's work centers on identifying the feature (or features) of a company that creates value. If you are an owner interested in improving your company's competitive advantage, I recommend that you read one of Dr. Porter's books. Or you might seek the counsel of one of the 2,080,000 companies or individuals that appeared when I recently conducted an online search for "competitive advantage consultants."

But there was more to my search than simply identifying a company's competitive advantage, and I suspected that leverage was related to the relationship between the buyer and the seller. Is there something about the relationship between what the seller has to sell and the impact the seller has on the buyer? Does the *sale process* that we use in these transactions produce an Outrageous Price?

At about this time, the red-hot mergers and acquisitions (M&A) market started to cool. Tight credit and economic uncertainty increased the number of aborted transactions, and potential sellers grew justifiably wary of investment bankers promising solid, much less outrageous, sale prices.

My focus necessarily turned to creating a process that would stack the deck in my clients' favor. I describe that process, the Proactive Sale Strategy, in Part One (the first five chapters) of this book.

When the M&A market is percolating, it is not difficult to get good prices for good companies, but even then it is the Proactive Sale Strategy that lays the groundwork to transform a good price into an outrageous one and maximizes a seller's probability of closing.

In less certain market conditions (or especially when there is a multitude of sellers and few buyers), not only does the Proactive Sale Strategy reduce the very real risk of a buyer walking away from the transaction to find greener pastures, but it is the key to obtaining the best possible—and on occasion outrageous—price.

As you read this book, I think some of the emotional reasons that prompted me to embark on a career in investment banking will become clear. First, there's a little larceny in my heart. I freely admit that I take great pleasure in getting an owner $8 million for his or her company from a buyer rather than $4 million. I get a kick out of making my clients lots of money. I knew going into this career that figuring out how to make money for clients gets my juices flowing, but I didn't anticipate that it would lead to a book.

Second, I love gamesmanship. I relish the intricate planning that goes into setting the stage for a transaction and into the timing and precision of delivering carefully scripted lines. I revel in the fact that there's rarely a predictable plotline to the Outrageous Price Process and that I must deftly and extemporaneously handle the many personalities and problems that inevitably arise. (We'll discuss both personalities and problems later in this book.)

But perhaps what I enjoy most is that the Proactive Sale Strategy and the Outrageous Price Process demand both right-brain intuition and left-brain analysis. There's no way to successfully orchestrate both processes without the two sides firing in perfect synchronization. That excitement keeps me coming to work each day, pausing to refine my hypotheses, and spending my remaining free moments writing a book.

When you complete this book, I hope you will share my excitement about the possibility of not only closing a sale successfully, but getting an Outrageous Price for your company. I also hope you'll understand that I'm not a guy who's been walking around for years hoping to write the next great business book. I'm not an academic; I'm in the marketplace doing deals because I make a great living doing it and because I love the process. My hope is that by the time you turn the last page, you'll see your company and its prospects for sale in a whole new light. If I can do that, I've succeeded.

Kevin M. Short

PART
1

The Proactive Sale Strategy

Laying the Foundation for a Sale

1

Reducing Seller Risk and Increasing Sale Proceeds

By and large, business owners are a schizophrenic group. When starting their companies, they put everything they own on the line. Typically, they pour into their companies every dime of their personal funds, pledge their family homes, and borrow from family members and banks, fully confident in their ability to pay off those loans. Even though they risk financial destruction (and often divorce) in doing so, they readily accept overwhelming odds as part of the package.

When it comes to selling their companies, however, owners have little stomach for risk. Having devoted heart, soul, and nearly every waking moment to nurturing their companies, few are confident about or eager to cash in their chips and walk away.

OBSTACLES TO SELLING A BUSINESS: REAL AND IMAGINED

In my career as an investment banker, I meet successful business owners every day who are, at some level, thinking about how they will jump off the locomotives that their businesses have become. But they hesitate—some for good reason: Their companies are simply unprepared for sale. Typically, "unprepared" means that without the owner's involvement, the company's continued profitability is uncertain at best. These owners have failed to install the systems and management teams that enable a successor owner to operate the company successfully.

So let's set aside the group of owners who justifiably hesitate to sell because they have not done the planning necessary to create saleable companies, and let's instead focus on another group.

In this group, we find owners who have saleable companies but believe that they cannot sell their companies today (or anytime soon) because the economy is too uncertain, buyers have fled the marketplace, and/or the buyers who remain are bottom-feeders willing to pay only bargain-basement prices.

Let's, for the moment, assume that all three of these boogeymen—the uncertain economy, the Ghosts of Buyers Past, and bottom-feeders—are real and are crouched and ready to pounce on owners naive enough to put their companies on the market. How then do we account for the sales that do happen—even in a tough economy? Further, how do we explain the fact that some companies are not only selling at healthy prices but selling at what I call *Outrageous Prices*?

I define an Outrageous Price as one that is at least two times the EBITDA multiple of an average company in its industry. While less common than during the heyday of the M&A market, even today there are real buyers paying Outrageous Prices for ordinary companies. Why and how does that happen? These questions fascinate me, and I share in this book some of the answers I've discovered.

Please don't misunderstand me: I applaud owners of saleable companies who are hesitant to enter the marketplace, to a point. I agree that owners do well to think twice about selling their companies, but not because of the current state of the economy or the presence of bottom-feeders. Bottom-feeders are all-season creatures, and the economy has always been and will always be cyclical.

I believe owners should think carefully before putting their companies on the market because without careful preparation a hefty percentage of companies put on the market will never sell. According to an Ernst & Young press release, "M&A conversion rates are at their lowest point for a decade. For transactions announced in the last nine months, only 60% by volume and 42% by value went on to complete in the same period" ("Global announced M&A deals rise in Q4 2012, but conversation rates continue to decline," London, 20 December 2012, www.ey.com/GL/en/Newsroom/News-releases/Global-announced-M-And-A-deals-rise-in-Q4-2012).

It is worth noting that the average deal value in the report (during the fourth quarter of 2012) was $231 million. The presence of very large transactions in the marketplace overstates the success rate for smaller companies. Bigger deals enjoy better odds of closing because there are usually several buyers vying to make the purchase and, often, the deals are worked out before the company ever goes on the market. In fact, there is an assumption that the big deals will close.

That's not the assumption in smaller deals. While transactions of any size can fail to close for a number of reasons (many of which are discussed in Chapter 3), here are several of the primary reasons deals in the midmarket fail:

- Sellers expect too high a price.
- If significant change in the selling company occurs, rarely is it able to quickly regain its balance.
- Buyers in this marketplace are harder to find.
- Family dynamics (common in this segment of the market) can work against a successful closing.

Large sellers have an army of analysts (and usually minute-to-minute stock prices) to set sale prices, so they rarely go into a transaction with unrealistic saleprice expectations. On the other hand, owners of midmarket companies must rely on a competent and experienced investment banker to align their expectations of value with that of the marketplace.

In addition, mid- and lower-middle-market companies are more vulnerable to significant internal changes than are large companies. In a midmarket company, the death of a CEO is a certain deathblow to a sale transaction. In contrast, large companies have succession plans in place and a stable of talent that reassure buyers who react with a yawn or a simple adjustment to the payment of the purchase price.

As implied earlier, large companies generally enter the marketplace with several buyers waiting at the negotiating table or eager to pull up a chair. Not so for mid- and lower-middle-market companies. Chapter 5 of this book is devoted entirely to how to locate, interest, and eventually sell midmarket companies to qualified buyers.

Finally, there are a number of family-owned businesses in the middle market. Without planning, family dynamics can torpedo a deal before we even have a chance to pull up the gangway. Even with careful planning, delicate relationships in family-owned businesses must be handled with extreme care if a deal is to close.

When one considers that the conversion rate for middle-market and lower-middle-market deals likely falls well short of 60 percent, the reluctance of owners in these marketplaces to sell makes sense. Sellers have a great deal to lose if they put their companies on the market and fail to close the deal. Losses can include any of the following:

- Customers, employees, and vendors
- Fees paid to advisers
- The cost of the owner's inattention to running the company
- The owner's personal disillusionment

In my mind, this list is far scarier—and more deadly—than the boogeymen that keep most potential sellers awake at night.

Loss of Customers, Employees, and/or Vendors

In an effort to gauge saleability and price, some owners decide to tell "just a few people" that the company is for sale or attempt to negotiate with an interested buyer without representation. In the first case, owners have no control over who learns about the contemplated sale. Employees, customers, vendors, and bankers all nurture and are connected to various grapevines, and all will likely react less than favorably to rumors of a sale.

Let's assume that employees, vendors, lenders, and customers don't abandon your ship when they hear your company is for sale. At a minimum, this juicy information will make them pause to locate the nearest exits. Competitors will do everything they can to exploit the uncertainty rumor of a sale creates to lead your customers and employees to their own greener pastures.

To owners who are tempted to go it alone or doubt the damage competitors can inflict, I relate the story of one owner (let's call him Fred) who called me after having been approached by a competitor about a possible sale. Fred had allowed the competitor (now acting as a potential buyer) to meet with his employees and customers. Within days of these meetings, the competitor/buyer began to hire Fred's best employees and steal his best customers. When Fred confronted his "buyer," it coolly informed Fred that it was no longer interested in pursuing the transaction. Too late, Fred realized that this competitor had never had a genuine interest in pursuing a purchase.

Loss of Adviser Fees

More cautious owners spend thousands of dollars to hire investment bankers to take their companies to market. Some bring in their attorneys to perform presale due diligence, and most ask their accountants to straighten out and audit their financial records. During the several months that it may take an investment banker to discover there's no suitable buyer interested in purchasing the company, the owner has paid that investment banker a hefty up-front fee and monthly retainers. That's as good a reason as any to pause before leaping into the market.

Cost of the Owner's Lack of Focus

Harder to calculate, but no less damaging, is the price companies pay as their owners spend more time (and energy) thinking about and working on a sale than they do on maintaining the company's profitability. The Proactive Sale Strategy takes about eighteen months to execute, and the time frame for a well-structured, well-planned sale (from the date the owner hires an investment banker to closing) is between eight and twelve months. If those time frames are longer than you expected, consider that the sale process for owners who enter it armed only with the hope that the right buyer will appear can last years, assuming the transaction closes at all.

Owner Disillusionment

It is not uncommon for owners to retain investment bankers after they have either attempted—unsuccessfully—to negotiate a transaction themselves or used an inexperienced adviser. Remember Fred's story? After the last phone call with his competitor, both Fred and his remaining employees were completely demoralized. Fred's loss of faith in the sale process convinced him that he was stuck in his company forever. This loss of faith and subsequent belief that one can never sell makes it especially difficult for owners to rebuild their management teams and regain momentum.

An owner's loss of faith in the sale process is similar to the loss of faith in the justice system that an innocent person might experience after having been convicted due to incompetent legal advice. In either case, the wronged parties must regroup and use exactly the system they now distrust to regain what they are due (their freedom or a reasonable purchase price).

In the face of these real risks—and the perpetual presence of bottom-feeders and a cyclically uncertain economy—what can owners who want or need to sell within the next year do to not only close the deal, but close it at the best possible price? I'm so glad you asked.

WHAT NOW?

I've spent the last twenty-plus years of my career immersed in bringing together sellers and buyers. During the market's heyday, the high tide raised all (or nearly all) boats, yet two nearly identical companies might sell for two radically different multiples. In the heat of battle, I could do no more than resolve to think about this observation at a future date. I've taken that time over the past several years.

In the cool objectivity of hindsight, I've reviewed the deals in which buyers paid at least twice the EBITDA multiple of an average company in its industry. I tested the possibility that a company that sold for twice the multiple of similar companies did so because the company was inherently outrageous: It had discovered a cure for cancer or the eat-all-you-want diet pill. That proved untrue. Most of these "outrageous" companies were quite ordinary, and, generally, their owners did not realize that what they were doing differently could be very valuable to certain buyers.

I then looked at the buyers who paid these Outrageous Prices; maybe they were outrageously naive. Since most of them are and were major corporations with legions of expert negotiators working on their behalf, that hypothesis did not hold water.

Then what was it?

After reviewing the details of numerous transactions in the middle market, I discovered what makes one company sell at twice the price of a similar company. I've tested my hypothesis and can now describe a two-part process that we can use not only to reduce the risk of not closing (in difficult markets when sellers far outnumber buyers), but also to secure the best possible—and sometimes even outrageous—sale price.

THE PROACTIVE SALE STRATEGY

I've named the rigorous process I use to position a company to sell to a well-financed buyer at the best possible price the *Proactive Sale Strategy* (PSS). Prospective sellers engage in this process *before* putting their companies on the market. The PSS reduces the seller's risk of not closing by putting energy, resources, and effort—in advance of any sale—into:

◆ Understanding the seller's asset
◆ Identifying and remediating any issues that could prevent a sale
◆ Uncovering (and often enhancing) the company's competitive advantage
◆ Identifying prospective buyers

In its concentration on the buyer's needs, and in other ways that we'll discuss later, the PSS is different from every other sale process out there.

Let's look at each step of the Proactive Sale Strategy briefly, then in more detail in the chapters that follow.

Step One: Assessing Sale Readiness

Entering into any endeavor before one is ready can, and usually does, end in disaster. Consider the hiker who ventures into the wilderness without adequate supplies or equipment, or the student who sits down to a final exam without having opened a book. Not as common a nightmare, perhaps, but one with disastrous financial consequences is the owner who enters the M&A marketplace without careful preparation.

For that reason, our first step in the PSS is to ask an owner to answer a multitude of questions designed to assess how prepared the company—and the owner—is for sale. We probe several important areas, including the owner's exit goals, exit strategy awareness, family considerations, advisers, company systems, competitors, potential buyers, industry acquisition activity, and competitive advantage.

We need to know what expectations owners have about their exits and then ask if various constituency groups within the company (such as other owners or key managers) share those expectations. We take a quick snapshot of the advisers an owner is already using, before diving into all of a company's systems with an eye to understanding how transferable, scalable, and reproducible they are.

We then look at a company's environment: its competitors, possible buyers, and current acquisition activity in its industry. Finally, we take a second look at the company's systems to determine which one(s) might make the company different from its competitors and thus valuable to a buyer.

Step Two: Presale Due Diligence

In this step, we dissect all the information we collected and analyzed in step one. The owner's answers to our sale readiness questions guide us as we put the company under a microscope to see if it can withstand the scrutiny of a buyer's due diligence. Buyers pry open every dark closet and turn every stone before taking a seat at the closing table. For that reason, not only must owners reveal to us every skeleton in every closet; we must remove those skeletons or minimize their potential negative impact upon the buyer. Preparing for due diligence *before* the sale process begins saves time during the sale process and thus reduces the risk of a failure to close.

Step Three: Identify the Competitive Advantage

Again in step three we turn to the preliminary information about the company that we collected in step one. As you know, a competitive advantage is the product a company makes or the service it offers either better or more cheaply than its competitors—over time. In the context of the Proactive Sale Strategy, however, we are looking for an existing, or potential, fit between the seller's competitive advantage and the buyer's need. Better yet—and absolutely critical to getting an Outrageous Price for a company—we are searching for a way that the seller's company (1) can (or could, if given time and preparation) meet a buyer's immediate need or (2) could pose an imminent threat to a buyer.

Step Four: Identify the Buyers

At this point in the process we focus our attention on potential buyers in the marketplace. Our goal is to identify which companies in the M&A marketplace can use their significantly greater resources (such as access to capital, more efficient processes, deeper or wider distribution channels, or massive sales force) to make more money from a company than can its current owner. Identifying the potential buyer, or possibly buyers, takes a huge amount of research but pays equally huge dividends, as it significantly reduces a seller's risk of not closing.

Once we have identified the buyer(s) that could benefit most from acquiring a company, we gather competitive intelligence about these buyers. We look for information about:

◆ Past acquisitions
◆ Prices paid
◆ Changes in strategic acquisition plans
◆ Problems they may be encountering in their industries
◆ Changes in their industry position or reputation
◆ Personnel changes
◆ Changes in their regulatory environment

We'll use that information about a buyer's preferences and behavior (if we engage in the Outrageous Price Process) to map a strategy to make that buyer aware of the value in the acquisition. We'll talk about ways to inject awareness of the seller's company into the consciousness of the selected buyers in Chapter 7.

Once we have determined how to catch the buyer's eye, we can actively, yet anonymously, engage the prospective buyer. When investment bankers engage potential buyers, they contact representatives of each prospective buyer on a seller's behalf without revealing the selling company's identity. Owners simply cannot maintain their confidentiality when representing themselves.

As the relationship between the transaction intermediary and potential buyer grows, we learn more specific details about what a buyer typically pays for companies in the seller's industry, who its negotiators are, what attributes it looks for, and what problems it commonly encounters. We use this information so that when the seller announces its intent to sell, it does so with all its ducks in a row.

The Proactive Sale Strategy reduces a seller's risk of failing to close the deal, but it also increases the seller's chances for getting the sale price he or she wants—even in a tough M&A market. It does so by carefully preparing the seller's company, aligning the seller's assets to the buyer's needs, and understanding and acting upon the buyer's priorities and preferences.

Let's look at each step in more detail, beginning with step one: assessing sale readiness.

2

Step One: Assess the Company and Owner for Sale Readiness

T ake your mark, get set, go! How many childhood games start with these words? While selling your company in a tough market at the best possible price is not a game for children, for the uninitiated, or for the weak of heart, it is a game. It is a game with multiple players, identifiable winners and losers, and a fluid set of rules. But just because you have played other games (such as running a successful company) with ease, expertise, and finesse, that doesn't necessarily mean you are prepared to play the game of selling your company for an Outrageous Price.

I compare an owner's entry into the transaction arena to experiences we've all had at some point growing up. Remember being the new kid in a new classroom in a new school? Or the time when the big kids asked you to join a neighborhood pickup game? You'd been in a classroom for years or played the game hundreds of times, and, up to this moment, you knew every player, every rule, every nuance, and every exception. But in this new situation you are uncertain. You don't know the rules or the players. Which kid plays rough? Which kid wilts under pressure? Who are the smart kids, the thugs, and the brownnosers? What are the consequences for picking the wrong group, checking the wrong player, or being a hot dog? You watch, you listen, and you tentatively play according to the "old" rules. Maybe things go well for a while until you break a rule you didn't know existed. Consequences are swift and vary in severity.

Remember feeling something between uneasy and scared or choosing between flight and fight? That choice or feeling in the pit of your stomach is not one you want to experience when you sell your company. Those feelings don't always contribute to being and playing your best. When selling your company, you want to feel the way you did when one of the other kids explained the spoken and unspoken rules, helped you navigate the personalities and avoid obstacles, and ultimately fed you the shot for the win.

When I represent owners, I try to be that kid—the one who helps the new kid understand enough about what's going on to not only survive, but to win. I call the process I use to help new kids, or owners, win this high-stakes game the Proactive Sale Strategy. Not only does this strategy maximize the owner's chance of finishing the game; it also maximizes the owner's chances of closing for the best possible—and even Outrageous—price.

In step one of this process, we begin with a valuation and comprehensive checkup of both the seller and the seller's company. Before entering the game, we want to understand exactly what the owner brings to the starting line.

I divide step one into two parts: market valuation and the Sale Readiness Assessment. The purpose of the valuation is fairly straightforward: We gather the information necessary to predict the average price a buyer would pay for a company in this industry, in its current condition, and at this moment in the M&A cycle. Using a Sale Readiness Assessment, we determine how prepared the company and owner are for a sale.

In most cases, we work to complete the valuation while the owner completes our Sale Readiness Assessment.

MARKET VALUATION

If you are like the hundreds of owners of companies in the middle market that I've met or represented over the past twenty-five years, you are successful, creative, and driven and you believe that you have a pretty good idea of the value of your company. With all due respect for your business acumen, I suggest that you do not.

Before you assume that I have insulted you and toss this book without reading another page, let me assure you that not knowing the value of your company does not mean that you are out of touch with your industry or the inner workings of your company. Rarely is anyone as attuned to all of a company's strengths and weaknesses as is its owner.

There are a number of reasons, however, why owners do not, and, I submit, should not, know the value of their companies. The first is that as valuations are traditionally performed, the purpose for the valuation significantly influences the resulting valuation or enterprise value. Second, commonly used assumptions that underlie valuations of privately held companies (and that's how most lower- to middle-midmarket companies are owned) are inexact, at best. Third, privately held companies exist in a world devoid of empirical data. And, finally, the input owners or sellers receive from potential buyers—input I refer to as *buyerspeak*—is carefully designed to cloud and deflate an owner's idea of value. (We'll talk more about buyerspeak in Chapter 5.)

Let's look at each of the flaws inherent in the valuation process in more detail.

Flaw #1: What's the Purpose of the Valuation?

If you've had a professional (accountant, business appraiser, investment banker) place a value on your company, you know that one of the first questions you are asked is: What is the purpose of the valuation?

Before we discuss how your answer affects the resulting valuation, let's pause to examine the question: Why do you want to know the value of your company? The very fact that you are asked to declare—up front—why you want the valuation performed indicates that your answer has a direct bearing on the process's outcome. Could that mean that professionally established valuations may not be the objective be-alls and end-alls that many assume them to be?

In pointing out that the motive for a valuation influences its result, I am not questioning the professionalism or skills of those who perform valuations or the validity of the reasons owners wish to have values put on their companies. Indeed, owners have legitimate reasons for valuations, but understand that a valuation appropriate for one purpose is not appropriate for all.

Owners require valuation information when they create and update buy/sell agreements or estate plans. The accountants or business appraisers who perform the valuations want to be aware of the owner's motives so that they can create valuation formulas that treat fairly both the departing and the remaining shareholders. In the case of a valuation performed for estate planning purposes, the valuation expert places the lowest defensible value on the company so that the owner's heirs will pay no more taxes than required.

Many owners want to know the value of their companies as part of creating their exit plans from their companies. To this end, they seek to determine if a sale, today or at a chosen time in the future, will provide them with financial freedom. Most owners include "achieve financial freedom" somewhere on their lists of "reasons I own my own company." While some owners go into business with that priority at the top of their lists, others place more emphasis on it as they age, as their priorities change, or as market conditions change. For example, when the merger and acquisition market is paying top dollar, owners who may not have considered selling decide that they can't afford *not* to sell. Or when economic conditions become more challenging, some owners simply tire of fighting tooth and nail for smaller margins.

We'll talk more in a moment about how valuations for sale purposes may not be as solid as we often assume them to be, but let's first complete our discussion about the problems inherent in any valuation.

Flaw #2: Faulty Assumptions

In addition to a valuation number being dependent on the reasons the valuation is conducted, valuations typically rely on wildly imprecise assumptions. The two biggest offenders are rules of thumb and multiples. Valuation specialists examine and analyze a company's financial statements, but they then factor in a generalization or rule of thumb to arrive at an enterprise value. For example, they may observe that in a particular industry, buyers "historically pay one times sales." Historically, that rule of thumb may or may not be true, but due to the lack of reliable data in this marketplace of privately held companies, we just don't know.

The second weakness inherent in any valuation made to predict a purchase price is the multiple. Simply put, a multiple is the rate of return that buyers expect on their investment. So, if buyers traditionally pay "a five multiple," this means that they expect a 20 percent annual return on their investment. On its face, that's a fairly straightforward statement until we consider that 20 percent of the purchase price doesn't factor in the postclosing benefits the buyers will experience from their expansion plans (made possible by their acquisition of the seller), the synergies between the two companies, or the expertise of the new management team.

Flaw #3: Lack of Empirical Data

It would be great if we could look at a past transaction and agree on exactly what the multiple meant in that particular situation. But we can't. We're operating in the privately held market, where information about sale transactions is difficult to find even with professional assistance. And that absence of reliable data is the third major flaw in the valuation process.

If you own a company worth between $10 million and $200 million, you occupy a spot in the no-man's-land known as the "lower middle market," where, according to the U.S. Census Bureau's latest numbers (2007), there are 803,356 firms (http://www.census.gov/epcd/www/smallbus.html). Hoover's (a Dun & Bradstreet company) calculates that there are 1,068,848 companies with listed revenue between $5 million and $200 million. Business owners in this market lack the accurate information about the value of their companies that is available to owners at both ends of the value spectrum.

Sellers of these middle-market companies are in no rush to share information about the sales of their companies. There is no advantage to them in disclosing the details about these transactions. The same is true of their public company buyers. When public companies buy middle-market companies, the purchase prices are often too small to rise to the level of materiality, so the buyers never need report them.

At one end of the value spectrum are large publicly traded companies. Every time one share of their stock changes hands, the market establishes a precise—albeit temporary—value for that company. At the other end of the spectrum, the market places a definite value on small items. For example, online auctions put a value on everything from stylish powder-blue leisure suits from the 1970s to collections of lawn trolls.

Privately held companies not only lack the exact values assigned to public companies, but they are too valuable and complex for any online auction. For that reason, the method of predicting a sale price is similar to that of diagnosing a condition such as Alzheimer's disease.

When called upon to make a diagnosis, medical doctors rely on observations about changes in the patient's personality, memory, judgment, abstract thinking, or ability to perform familiar tasks. While physicians do use blood tests and various types of brain scans, they do so to rule out other potential causes of dementia. The only way to achieve 100 percent accuracy in the Alzheimer's diagnosis is to perform a postmortem examination of the patient's brain.

Investment bankers face similar obstacles in predicting a sale price. They can carefully analyze a company's financial statements and make educated assumptions about the health of the M&A market, the future performance of the company, and the willingness of buyers to assume risk. Their estimates of a sale price, however, cannot be 100 percent certain until the transaction is completed. If we could only see the future or read the mind of the buyer (or buyers) in the marketplace, owners would know exactly what buyers are willing to pay and thus would know with certainty the true value of their companies.

VALUATION PROCESS

So let's review: Valuations of middle-market, privately held companies are (1) significantly affected by the purpose for the valuation, (2) usually based on faulty assumptions, and (3) performed in a vacuum of reliable data. At this point, many owners justifiably wonder exactly why they need a valuation and are convinced that their money would be better spent on lottery tickets.

Well, if we return to our analogy that selling a company is somewhat like a game, players (in this case, owners) must have the best possible understanding of the asset they bring to the starting line. Failure to do so significantly increases the risk that they'll not make it to the finish line—that is, the transaction will fail or they'll lose by failing to get the best possible price for the company.

As you recall, the two primary purposes of the Proactive Sale Strategy are to (1) reduce the seller's risk of a failure to close and (2) achieve the best possible sale price. One way we improve the seller's chances of success on both fronts is to match the seller's asset to a buyer's need. But if we don't understand the value of the seller's asset, how can we make that match, much less get the best possible sale price?

We can't.

But just because we reject *valuation formulas* based on questionable rules of thumb and hearsay doesn't mean that it is impossible to design a *valuation process* that combines rigorous analysis with the expertise and intuition of the professional performing the valuation. The sections that follow describe the valuation process that we use in the Proactive Sale Strategy.

Analysis of the Financial Statements

We begin our valuation process with a review of a company's most recent profit and loss statements and balance sheets. Ideally, we review both reports for each of the past three years so we can spot trends and anomalies and confirm that any change to the balance sheet flows through to the profit and loss statement.

We start with an assumption that a company's financial reports are accurate. That assumption is easiest to make if an owner provides us with audited financial statements. If audited, we know that (1) a certified public accountant has created these statements, (2) he or she agrees with the methods the company used to prepare the documents, and (3) the audit is accurate and complete.

One step below audited financials (in terms of credibility) is the unaudited financial statement. Here there are two levels: reviewed and compiled. When CPAs review a company's statements, they check certain items (such as accounts receivable and the methods for recording inventory) according to a predetermined routine. These routine checks are less stringent than ones used in an audit, and they do not include a review for accuracy of every number that the company provides. The CPA may, however, make one or more assurances about the reliability of the data.

In compiled statements, the CPA accepts all the company-provided data and puts it into a standardized format designed to tell the story of the company's financial performance. In compiled statements, the CPA expresses no opinion and makes no assurances about the accuracy of the data the company provides.

With financials in hand, we can begin the process of adjusting the numbers to reflect what each would be *if the company were owned by someone else*. For example, if the selling owner has taken a $2 million bonus, thus reducing the company's profit to $0, we ask what salary could we pay a similarly skilled person to do the owner's job? If that salary is $250,000, we add back $1,750,000 to the company's adjusted EBITDA.

We find these add-backs primarily in three areas: owner perks, onetime events, and typical trouble spots. Let's start with the most glamorous area:

owner perks. In this category we find country club dues, tickets to sporting events or theater subscriptions, and slope-side or beachfront condos. We see higher-than-possibly-justifiable salaries and the purchase and maintenance of vehicles of all kinds: boats, race cars, recreational vehicles, and airplanes.

Often, we discover that owners have had their businesses perform expensive services (such as building a home, remodeling a basement, landscaping a yard) at the business's expense. Again, if a replacement owner could be hired and satisfied to work without these high-dollar trimmings, we add back their costs.

Onetime events are typically not so glamorous because they include natural and human-caused disasters. On the natural side, we find casualty events such as fire or flood. On the human-caused side, litigation is the most common event that can skew a company's numbers. Of course, if a company is consistently involved in litigation, then we would not add back litigation-related costs.

Finally, we get to the most common yet hardest-to-define area: trouble spots. These spots are usually industry related. For example, if a company maintains a significant inventory, we know that this is the easiest place for an owner to massage the numbers. Here's how one owner massaged the numbers in a shortsighted attempt to reduce his tax liability.

> Vince Diamond owned a successful plumbing parts company in Detroit, Michigan. For years, Vince had understated his inventory in an effort to reduce his profits, thus reducing his tax liability. Vince provided the doctored numbers to his accountant, who, year after year, used them to prepare the company's tax returns.
>
> At Vince's fiftieth birthday party, his youngest son (who Vince had always hoped would take over the business) announced his plan to attend medical school. Vince's employees had neither the money nor the will to take over the company, so Vince decided to investigate the option of selling to a third party.
>
> During Vince's first meeting with a business broker, the broker questioned Vince's stated inventory of $250,000. "How can you possibly support annual sales of $2.5 million with an inventory this small?"
>
> Vince then admitted how, unbeknownst to his accountant, he had cleverly "saved hundreds of thousands" in taxes over the years by understating his inventory.

"Well," his broker said, "now you face a difficult choice. We can correct your inventory numbers so that your EBITDA will support a $10 million sale price."

"Great! Let's do it!" Vince replied.

"If we do," the broker cautioned, "the IRS can, and probably will, charge you with tax fraud."

Once Vince had absorbed and rejected that idea, he asked, "What happens if I let the numbers stand?"

The broker replied, "In that case, I have good news and bad news. The good news is that you don't go to jail. The bad news is that, without correcting the numbers, your company's EBITDA is too low to support a $10 million sale price. In fact, no buyer will risk buying a company with unsupportable numbers."

Dejected, Vince left the broker's office. He ran the company for eight more years until he had enough money in the bank to support himself in his retirement. At the end of those eight years, Vince liquidated what assets he could and closed the doors.

Another trouble spot appears in companies that use assets whose depreciation schedules exceed the assets' useful life. For example, if a company has significant investments in technology (computers, software, and peripherals), we look carefully at the validity of its depreciation schedule. For example, if a company purchases fifty new laptop computers for its sales staff, those laptops are assumed to have a useful life of five years and are therefore depreciated over five years. Let's assume that in year four the owner of this company decides to sell. We often discover that in year three the company replaced those fifty laptops with newer technology, yet they remain on the company's balance sheet. We must deduct the undepreciated amount (on assets the company no longer possesses) from the EBITDA so the company's profitability is not inflated.

We also often find issues to resolve concerning the ownership of real estate. One occurs when the company owns real estate inside the corporation. In this situation, companies usually do not pay rent, so we must show what rent would cost the company if it were owned outside the company. For sale purposes, we value the real estate separately from the company because the cash flow multiple for real estate exceeds the multiple for business cash flow.

The second issue occurs when real estate is owned by one or more of the company's principals and rented to the company. There is often a discrepancy between prevailing market rates and that paid by the principals. Some owners charge less than market rates, while others charge more. In either case, we adjust the EBITDA to reflect the difference between the rate the company pays and market rates.

Normalizing the Financial Statements

Once we have adjusted the numbers to best reflect what the company is worth, we can normalize the financial statements. *Normalize* means comparing the selling company with others in the same industry and of similar size. We want to know if the selling company uses the same methodologies in preparing its financial statements as do others in its industry. For example, let's assume two companies show the same amount for the cost of goods sold. If one company includes some direct labor components when it computes the cost of goods and its industry competitor does not, the financial reports will tell two different stories.

The final step in the analytical half of our valuation process is to collect (using a number of proprietary databases) information about recent sales in the industry. This process parallels the one a real estate agent uses to develop a list of comparative properties before setting an asking price. While we may not be able to uncover exact purchase prices for privately held companies, we can discover what buyers are active in the marketplace, how active they are, and what types of acquisitions they make. If we discover that buyers have abandoned a particular market, we can make the appropriate adjustment to our valuation.

Intuition/Judgment

In this second half of our valuation process, we draw upon experience, training, and intuition to probe any anomalies we find in the company-provided data, the owner-provided information, or the information regarding sales in the industry. We ask questions about any discrepancies between what the data indicate and what owners tell us.

One item that requires a judgment call is a variation on the onetime event anomaly mentioned earlier. For example, a company may encounter a spike in the cost of fuel or in one of its primary input commodities. If the price of that input has returned to a normal level and we do not foresee another spike, we recast the company's numbers as if the spike had never occurred. We do that so a future owner has a better appreciation of this company's normal performance. If, on the other hand, we believe that the price increase or fluctuation is likely to recur, we would not treat it as an add-back because fluctuations of this kind are part of this company's ordinary business activity.

Analysis + Intuition = Valuation Process

The combination of keen analysis and intuition based on years of experience yields our opinion of a company's current and possible range of value. "Current" relates to existing acquisition activity in the marketplace and availability of credit. Our estimates of "possible" cover a range but do not include the amount that the best possible buyer might be induced to pay under the best possible conditions (aka the Outrageous Price). Although the very purpose of the Proactive Sale Strategy and Outrageous Price Process is to find that best possible buyer and *prepare that buyer* to pay the highest possible price, at this point we do not include the Outrageous Price in our range of value.

In contrast to a formal valuation report, our opinion of value is not a written report, so if owners are at all pleasantly or unpleasantly surprised with our opinion, we encourage them to secure a formal valuation report. Doing so is critical if there are minority owners involved who may, at some point, wish to question the majority owner's decision to agree to a purchase price.

We provide an opinion of a range of value to the owner *before we enter into an engagement* because designating the range of value puts owners at a crossroads. Knowing what they now know about current possible value, are they willing to sell for an amount within that range? As they consider that range, they must think about the probability of securing a price within the stated range. For example, we may be able to expect, with near certainty, that a buyer willing to pay $4 million will appear. The prospects for a sale are far fewer, however, at the $10 million end of the range.

SALE READINESS ASSESSMENT

As we analyze data pertinent to valuation, we begin the process of determining how ready an owner and the company are for sale. We conduct a full exam of the selling company, much like the executive physical exams performed on high-level business executives at major medical centers. Over the course of a day or two, doctors take measurements, palpate, observe, listen, and evaluate all the executive's systems, including hematological (blood chemistry and counts), respiratory (chest X-ray), digestive, excretory, reproductive, cardiovascular, and neurological. Doctors may also examine eyes, teeth, skin, diet, nutrition, and stress levels.

When we examine a company, the process is similar. While our "patient" is the company, we ask the owner to assume the role of its spokesperson and to answer each question to the best of his or her knowledge. Usually, those answers are based on the owner's intuition.

The investment banker's primary role in this assessment is to ask the right questions, listen carefully to an owner's answers, and draw upon experience, intuition, and training to begin to make conclusions.

We probe several important areas, including the owner's exit goals, exit strategy awareness, family considerations, advisers, company systems, competitors, potential buyers, industry acquisition activity, and competitive advantage. Appendix A is the Sale Readiness Assessment that my firm uses. Let's look at each assessment area in more detail.

Exit Goals

At the outset of this process, we want to know what owners expect from a sale. We ask owners to define their "ideal" sale in terms of price, timing, role after closing, role of employees after closing, feelings about possible reorganization of the company, and optimal personal tax ramifications.

It is often a cat-and-mouse moment when I ask owners to name both their ideal sale price and a realistic sale price. Owners don't know me well at this point, and they suspect that there's an advantage in having me name these prices first. Their suspicion that there's more to this question than meets the eye is correct, but by declaring their prices first, they do not put themselves at a disadvantage. My only (and up to now) hidden agenda is to use owners' answers to gauge their understanding of the company, industry, and marketplace. In reality, owners lose no advantage in revealing their price targets because in the end—*and at every point along the way to closing*—the owners (not their investment bankers) retain the power to accept or reject a buyer's offer.

While we probe owners' gross price expectations, we also want to know what form of payment they deem acceptable. Are they willing to accept a promissory note, stock of the buyer's company, royalties, earnouts, or other noncash arrangements? The answer guides future negotiations with buyers.

During the assessment we ask if there's a party (or parties) that an owner is unwilling to consider as a potential buyer. Several years ago I met with a seller who, during one of our first meetings, presented me with a list of companies he thought might be interested in buying his company. Noticeably absent from this list was his company's largest competitor. When asked about this omission, this seller told me he didn't trust the competitor and would not permit me to approach, much less negotiate with, this competitor. Whether this seller's feelings were well founded or not (and we later learned they were not) his veto had a profound effect on my estimate of the "average" sale price for this company. In one blow, the seller eliminated the buyer best able to pay the highest price.

We also spend time exploring the selling owner's role after the sale. Would he or she consider remaining as an employee? If so, for how long? At what rate of compensation? Or would the seller prefer a consulting arrangement? Would the seller prefer to work for a strategic buyer (probably a competitor) or for a group that remains at arm's length (a private equity group)? If required to sign a covenant not to compete, what terms does the seller deem acceptable and unacceptable?

Exit Strategy Awareness

We turn then to an owner's constituency groups. These may include other owners, a spouse, family members, a board of directors, senior management, and key employees. These are the critical questions for each group: Are these persons aware of the owner's ideal sale plan, and, if so, do they share the same vision?

An owner's answers to these questions give me insight into the amount of exit planning the owner has done and the culture of the organization. It is optimal (but not necessary) for owners to start planning their departures at least five years in advance of their exits. As part of the exit planning process, owners define their visions of the company's future and communicate those visions and plans to their constituency groups so that everyone works toward the same goal.

In my experience, however, few owners devote the time and effort necessary to create comprehensive exit plans, and fewer still share those exit plans with their employees. While the benefits of creating an exit plan are many, most owners (and most of their advisers) have no idea how beneficial exit plans are in both the short term and the long run.

Every exit plan is founded on a particular owner's goals, one of which is usually to reap as much cash as possible at exit. To accomplish this goal, a comprehensive exit plan includes specific actions to promote and protect business value. Promoting value typically involves owners installing various incentive programs that motivate key employees to both increase the value of their companies and remain with the companies—even after owners depart.

One technique that owners use to achieve this two-faceted goal is a *stay bonus plan*. It is so important that we'll digress from our discussion of sale readiness briefly to describe it.

The Stay Bonus Plan

An effective stay bonus plan accomplishes three tasks: (1) It gives the key managers a reason to stay with the company after the owner's exit, (2) it is structured so that it increases the value of the company, and (3) it includes a penalty (usually in the form of a covenant not to compete) that prevents key managers from taking customers, vendors, or trade secrets with them should they leave before or after the sale.

Owners who rely on their belief in their employees' goodwill rather than on written stay bonus plans often find themselves held hostage by those same good and loyal employees.

One owner was a week away from the sale of his company for $10 million when (at this very late stage of the game) the buyer met with each of the key managers to reassure them that they'd be retained by the new owners at their existing compensation levels. At its meeting with this owner's top salesperson, the buyer was lavish in praising her performance and indicated how important her continued success was to the company's future success. When the buyer then asked her to sign a covenant not to compete before the closing date, the salesperson asked for a short break and headed straight for the owner's office. She proceeded to remind him that she'd help build the company to its current value during her tenure and ever-so-generously consented to patiently wait until the closing date "to collect her $1 million bonus."

This owner paid the ransom because he knew that if this salesperson servicing his top four clients left the company, the buyer would likely scrap the deal. If the buyer did subsequently come to the closing table, it would reduce the purchase offer by far more than $1 million.

In another transaction, I was orchestrating the sale of a division of a publicly held company. We were conducting a competitive auction (see Chapter 10) and were introducing each of four possible buyers to the division CEO. At the meeting with the first buyer, the CEO was rude. I thought perhaps she was having an off day until she repeated the same behavior with the second buyer.

Before meeting our third buyer, she and I sat down so I could ask about her behavior. To my surprise, she informed me that she didn't like those prospective buyers and that it was critical that she like the people she'd be working for. She patiently explained to me, "If I pick the wrong buyer, I might be fired." I left that meeting and contacted her supervisors, and this CEO's premonition was fulfilled sooner than she expected: She was fired that afternoon.

In firing her, the parent company excised a thorn from its side, but that surgery cost it a third of its sale price. It found itself selling a division with a brand-new CEO and quickly learned that no buyer was willing to pay a premium for an untested manager.

As a result of these and many other all-too-similar experiences, I strongly recommend that owners engage in exit planning and implement stay bonus plans with anyone who has a significant impact on their company's performance. When considering which employees should qualify for stay bonuses, include anyone who has leverage against the company, and remember that among that group might be the janitor whose cousin is your biggest customer.

If you are interested in learning more about exit planning, I suggest that you visit www.exitplanning.com for unbiased information.

Family Business Considerations

In the course of my work, I meet with owners of family businesses who have decided to at least investigate, and often pursue, a sale to a third party. These owners arrive at their decisions for various reasons, most commonly one of these two: (1) Their children are unable or unwilling to succeed them, or (2) the next generation simply cannot match the price that a third party will pay for the company.

It is not uncommon for children to be unwilling or unable to step into ownership positions. Typically, the company that children are being asked to run is significantly larger and more complex than the one their fathers or mothers ran at their age. In addition, few hard-charging entrepreneurs are also skilled trainers of a second generation.

Rarely have I met an owner whose son or daughter shares his or her unique drive or talents. That's not surprising when you consider that the two generations are often raised in completely different environments. The parent entrepreneur likely had few parent-provided opportunities, while Junior has likely had many. Junior has watched Mom or Dad devote everything to the company and justifiably believes that "there must be an easier way to make a living."

The "kids don't have the money to pay for the company" roadblock is very common. While it is possible for family members to be able to match the price of a third-party buyer, this can take place only when the departing owner takes action years in advance of the transfer. Yes, years. It takes years to put in place the mechanisms that transfer ownership and management responsibilities in a way that ensures both the ongoing success of the company and the departing owner's postbusiness financial security.

If an owner decides that the time has come to exit and has not done the exit planning necessary to leave the company to children, that owner correctly views the sale to a third party as his or her best route to financial security.

Unfortunately, few owners verbalize to family members their evolution in thought from a transfer to children to a sale to a third party. Many owners talk for years about how their children will succeed them only to realize that a family transfer cannot meet all of their goals.

My job is to help owners understand how family members will react when they change horses midstream. Spouses, ex-spouses, and children (both those active in the business and those not active) will have strong opinions about a sale to a third party. Some owners have written succession plans but decide instead to sell to third parties. Other owners have offhandedly quipped to a son or daughter-in-law, "One day, all this will be yours." To the owner, that comment means nothing more than "Work hard, and I'll give you a chance to buy into the company." The listener more likely heard something about inheriting the company.

Family expectations, relationships, and communications are loaded with emotion. Family members can and often do oppose and derail sales to third parties. That's why it is so critical—before entering the marketplace—for owners to think carefully about all of the interested parties involved and work proactively to manage their expectations.

Company Advisers

In this part of our Sale Readiness Assessment, we want to know about a company's relationships with its lender(s) and advisers. Primarily, we want to know how strong the relationship is with the lender(s) and how experienced other advisers are in third-party transactions.

When owners describe their relationship with their bank as "poor" (usually peppering our conversation with words such as *demanding, unresponsive,* and *unrealistic*), we probe further. Often, but not always, we discover that a poor relationship between an owner and a banker is the result of the banker's lack of trust in company-provided numbers or a company's history of sporadic or late payments.

In terms of advisers, we are most interested in (and hope to influence) an owner's choice of transaction attorney because that attorney is so critical to the success of the process. Usually, owners have longtime relationships with a local law firm. They've used that firm to set up the corporate entity, draw up shareholder or buy/sell agreements, and perhaps write employment agreements or benefit program arrangements. What those attorneys may not do often, or at all, is participate in the type of sale process described in this book: one in which every actor's role is carefully scripted to yield the best possible, or Outrageous, price.

As I catalogue my experiences in securing the Outrageous Price, I notice that in almost every case I had the opportunity to refer the sellers to a short, carefully compiled list of attorneys who not only were the best at what we asked them to do (presale legal due diligence and creating documents that protect the seller), but could play well with others. In the cases where I did not handpick the attorney, the sellers picked attorneys who were excellent technicians but had no desire to run the deal process.

Achieving the best possible price or Outrageous Price requires teamwork. Attorneys who adopt a know-it-all attitude, fail to ask questions, or don't realize that their role is just one in an ensemble performance are impediments to the seller's goal. In fact, a difficult or belligerent attorney is more damaging to the process than is an incompetent one.

As you'll see in later chapters, pursuing the Outrageous Price is much like playing a high-stakes poker game. Players carefully watch each other for tells. The more experienced the players, the more subtle the tells and the more skill and sensitivity it takes to detect them. The last thing a player needs is distraction from the cocktail waitress or a spectator. In the pursuit of the Outrageous Price, the investment banker (your proxy at the table) doesn't know what cards the buyer will play so must devote full attention to the game. If an attorney distracts rather than supports your investment banker, you will walk away from the table with fewer chips.

The Company

In this largest section of the Sale Readiness Assessment, we attempt to learn as much as we can about the company's pricing, costs, employees, marketing plans, technology, business model, industry, customers, and, last but certainly not least, systems. The information we gather in this part of the assessment forms the basis for our presale due diligence in step two and competitive advantage analysis in step three.

But our questions in this step are unlike those we ask when performing presale due diligence in step two. For example, in this step when we question an owner about employees, we ask, "Do you know why your employees work for you?" "Do you know how happy they are working for you?" and "Do your employees affect your customers' purchase decisions?" By contrast, when we conduct presale due diligence in step three, we ask for names of employees, tenure with the company, resumes of key managers, employment contracts, and Equal Employment Opportunity Commission (EEOC) policies and infractions.

In short, the Sale Readiness Assessment complements the due diligence process in that the latter is document-heavy and requires right-brain analysis, while the former is softer and more intuitive. Not only does the Sale Readiness Assessment help us to determine if the owner is ready to sell, it provides the basis for the additional intelligent and targeted questioning necessary in the Outrageous Price Process.

Competitors

In this sixth area of our Sale Readiness Assessment, we seek the owner's insights into the company's competitors: who they are, whether the company has ever exploited a competitor's weakness, and if, in the owner's opinion, there is a competitor who might be a buyer. We also want to know if the owner knows why potential customers choose to buy from a competitor rather than from the owner's company. Finally, we want to know if the owner is aware of, and/or measures the company against, applicable industry standards.

Potential Buyers

Building on what we uncover about competitors, we ask the owner to list competitors, vendors, or others outside the company who might benefit from buying the company. If we anticipate that the buyer will be an industry player (as we often do in the Outrageous Price Process), owners generally are able to provide a very good list of possible buyers. On the other hand, if the company lacks the competitive advantage that we can leverage to cause a buyer tremendous gain or pain, your investment banker should do considerable research to create a comprehensive list of potential buyers. In either case, we want to know if the owner has any contacts in these organizations or is linked in any way to them.

Current Acquisition Activity

While any competent investment banker can gather data about acquisition activity in any industry, we want the owners to share with us their expertise and knowledge about any industry-specific valuation issues. We ask them whether they are familiar with any of the details of recent acquisitions, such as why buyers are making purchases, the form of payment they use (cash/note/equity), how much they are paying, and the size of acquisition they prefer. This is the type of information we'll collect from potential buyers as we prepare those buyers later in the Outrageous Price Process.

Competitive Advantage

Finally, we turn to questions related to a company's competitive advantage. We want owners' opinions about why customers buy from their companies rather than from their competitors. We ask owners if they have thought about developing a competitive advantage and for their ideas about how they could better position their companies to appeal to buyers.

This section of the Sale Readiness Assessment is the one that owners most often return unanswered, but, answered or unanswered, these questions provide the springboard for our discussion of competitive advantage in step three. If you are already scrambling (mentally, of course) to describe your company's competitive advantage, let me assure you that few owners can articulate exactly what it is that makes their customers choose their companies over their competitors. We'll talk more about how to uncover and exploit a competitive advantage in Chapters 4 and 6.

As you can see, the purpose of assessing sale readiness is to obtain a fairly detailed overview of the company and determine a likely sale price before entering the game (or going to market). With that information in hand, owners can decide to pursue a sale or return to their companies armed with information about how much they need to grow value, as well as specific ideas about how to do so.

For a complete list of questions contained in the Sale Readiness Assessment, please see Appendix A.

3

Step Two: Presale Due Diligence

In the first step of the Proactive Sale Strategy, we collected a wealth of information about the company, about sales in its industry, and about the owner. At the end of that collection process, the prospective seller has an opinion of value and marketability, and, based on the seller's answers to the questions in our Sale Readiness Assessment, we have an idea about his or her goals, potential opportunities, and threats.

At this point we meet to discuss what we've learned, clarify the reasons for the range of value we assigned to the company, and probe the likelihood of getting one sale price versus another.

This usually very candid discussion gives the owner information necessary to decide whether to pursue or postpone a sale, and it gives me an opportunity to gauge an owner's personality, habits, likes, and dislikes. All of these traits are important if we choose to work together toward a sale and, if all other parts are in place, is hugely important should we be able to pursue the Outrageous Price. (Please see Chapter 8 for a discussion of the character-istics of an Outrageous Owner.)

Let me insert here a brief comment about the relationship between the range of value and the owner's decision to sell or not sell. Suppose I tell an owner that I can sell his or her company for $10 million with 100 percent certainty or for $100 million with 10 percent certainty. The owner has a decision to make: Where along that continuum is he or she willing to sell?

The range I typically provide is rarely so broad—unless there's a possibility that there's a buyer who is willing to pay twice what all other buyers would (aka the Outrageous Buyer). Normally, I provide prospective sellers the bottom of the price range and am comfortable extending that range by one multiple. For example, I may be able to fix the bottom purchase price at a four multiple and the upper limit at the five multiple.

If the owner decides to pursue a sale within these parameters, it is time to dissect all the information we collected and analyzed in step one of the Proactive Sale Strategy. The company's financial information and the owner's answers in our Sale Readiness Assessment guide us as we put the company under a microscope during step two: presale due diligence, to see if both can withstand the scrutiny of a buyer's due diligence.

DUE DILIGENCE

Due diligence as a concept is simple: Buyers despise risk and do all they can to reduce it. So during due diligence buyers ask for every document that they deem necessary to assure themselves that the acquisitions they are considering are worth what the sellers represent them to be. To achieve that end, buyers look for any malfeasance or undisclosed material risk, such as fraud, on the part of the sellers or their managers. They look for items or issues the sellers aren't disclosing, such as unpaid taxes, pending or threatened litigation, or technical obsolescence of the company's equipment, processes, product, or service. Finally, buyers use due diligence to search for areas in which they can make immediate improvements (thus earning additional revenue) such as inefficiencies, unnoticed opportunities, waste, and mismanagement.

In this search, buyers request hard evidence for every claim that sellers make—from who owns the company to how many widgets it produces; from who owns the real estate on which it operates to who its customers are; from where it is licensed to do business to whether it is in compliance with all applicable regulations. If a buyer intends to arrive at the closing table with cash, the seller can be assured that on the way to the table the buyer will press the seller through its due diligence grinder.

And that's where the simplicity ends, because on the other end of this due diligence process are sellers—men and women who have put everything into their successful companies and are now involved in not only the most important financial transaction of their lives, but also one of the most emotional.

All sellers experience some anxiety about due diligence for one or more of several reasons:

1. The process of collecting and organizing data is a daunting task that many owners undertake on their own because they wish to keep confidential the prospect of a sale.
2. Most sellers do not understand the reasons for due diligence, so their assumptions about process take a significant emotional toll.
3. There are unscrupulous buyers who, with no intention of closing the deal, use due diligence to gather competitive intelligence about sellers.
4. For various reasons, the due diligence process has evolved into an enormous beast.

Before discussing how sellers can address each of these anxiety-inducing issues, let's examine them in greater detail.

Owners and Data

Most owners of midsize companies no longer create their own financial statements or organize and file every contract, bank statement, and license. They don't maintain or update their corporate documents; write all the checks; constantly update their lists of machinery, equipment, office furniture, and fixtures; keep a diary of all pending and past litigation; manage all regulatory compliance issues; keep track of every customer that has left; or consistently update the company's organizational chart (complete with up-to-date salaries, benefits, and job descriptions). Owners employ people who perform these tasks and can organize these items (and the many more on the due diligence lists in Appendix B and Appendix C). But once owners engage in negotiations with buyers, they must find, copy, organize, and, often, analyze all of these items:

- ◆ Without help from their employees. (Owners often decide to keep a transaction confidential until a closing is likely.)
- ◆ On a deadline. (Time favors buyers, so producing documents quickly is critical for sellers.)
- ◆ While continuing to operate their companies at peak performance. (Of course, there's no ideal time to experience a drop in revenues, but the period during which one is negotiating a sale is perhaps the least optimal.)

Realistically, owners working alone cannot collect all of the information on these lists. They must rely on, at a minimum, their chief financial officers (CFOs) for help. We prefer to work with sellers to craft stay bonus plans for those employees who will help with presale due diligence *before the process begins.* (See Chapter 2 for more details about these plans.) Once employees sign stay bonus plans, owners have greater assurance that these employees will work toward, not against, a sale.

Emotional Toll

At the risk of understating the point, owners don't like the due diligence process. Their reasons vary from the rational (collecting and organizing a small boatload of data demands time and energy that they could spend on their companies, their families, their hobbies, etc.) to the irrational ("These buyers want all this documentation because they doubt my integrity!")

> A number of years ago, I represented a seller of an office equipment company. Let's call him Liam O'Malley. We were on the eve of closing, when the buyer in this transaction made a very minor last-minute request that sent Liam into orbit. "That's it! No more! I've given in time and time again. Now they want me to pay the overnight shipping charges on documents they could have requested weeks ago! Forget it. I'm done."
>
> The history of this deal was like most: The buyer had asked for small concessions at every stage of the process. It was the cumulative effect of having to consider each request that aggravated Liam. Liam's anger had far more to do with the frequency of the requests than it did with their legitimacy. As we reviewed each request, it was clear that this buyer had

been very reasonable and had stayed in the deal despite the fact that we had denied most of its requests. When I pointed out that pattern to Liam, his emotional energy began to dissipate. Liam's fatigue stemmed from the emotion of the constant exchange, not from the quality of the deal.

Generally, integrity has little to do with buyers' requests unless they discover in their review of a seller's documents something that gives them cause. But keep in mind that buyers ask for all these documents *before* knowing anything about a seller. What buyers consider to be reasonable requests designed to decrease their risk, sellers often consider to be onerous and all-out attacks on their good character.

To bridge this huge gap of misunderstanding, we do two things with selling owners before the buyer's due diligence process even begins. First, we conduct a presale due diligence process to give sellers a small taste of what they will endure later in the process. In essence, we use presale due diligence like a vaccine. By injecting a small amount of the germ into healthy patients, we inoculate them against the disease.

Second, we remind owners that if they expect buyers to arrive at the closing table with a large check for a company they really know nothing about, they'd also better expect those buyers to do everything they can to reduce their risk of losing that cash. Ultimately, sellers have a choice about how they manage buyers' due diligence. Sellers can prepare for it, understand the reasons behind it (reducing the buyers' perception of risk), and pocket a sizeable amount of cash at closing. Or sellers can resist or refuse buyers' reasonable requests and subsequently pocket much smaller amounts of cash at the closing table—if they even get that far.

It is a transaction truism that buyers who are not confident in a seller's representations or who cannot verify the seller's claims bring less cash to closing. They may (or may not) pay the same amount as a confident buyer, but wary buyers shift much of the purchase price into earnouts. The lower the confidence level, the greater the earnouts and the amount of time that must elapse before they expire. (Please see the "Seller Concessions" section later in this chapter for more information about earnouts and how they work.)

Unfortunately, sellers often ignore my reminders, warnings, and explanations, as did Joseph Ritter (a fictional name for a real seller).

I met Ritter in May 2010 to represent him in the sale of his $25 million hunting goods wholesale company. At our second or third meeting,

I told Joe that the documents I needed to prepare the deal book for his company and to conduct presale due diligence would pale in comparison to what the buyer would ask for when conducting due diligence. Joe assured me that this wasn't his first rodeo and he'd do just fine. When I tried to share the same insights into due diligence that I do in this chapter, I could see Joe had tuned me out, so we moved on.

Six months after that conversation, I learned that Joe's previous "rodeo experience" of selling several homes didn't prepare him for the buyer's multiple requests for documents or for the size of his attorney's bills (reflecting the amount of time spent collecting and organizing those documents). Having expected the sale process to resemble a sale of real estate, Joe interpreted each buyer request as an attack on his integrity. He grew so agitated and obsessed with the process that his wife threatened divorce and his son in the business quit. At Joe's Thanksgiving dinner that year, there was tension in the air and several empty chairs at the table.

Competitive Intelligence Gathering

While most buyers use due diligence to reduce their risk, and there are indeed some who use it to methodically chip away at the purchase price, sellers worry most about those rare few who use due diligence to gather competitive intelligence with no intention of closing the deal. Sellers are so anxious about this possibility that at some point almost every seller I've worked with has suspected that the buyer was negotiating in bad faith. If a buyer postpones a scheduled meeting, asks for additional data, or sends an unexpected representative to a meeting, sellers often interpret those actions as proof of the buyer's nefarious intentions.

If sellers allow paranoia about a buyer's intentions to take root and color all of their decisions, their resulting behavior will drive the buyer away from the transaction. If they are not careful, sellers can easily create self-fulfilling prophecies.

Years ago, an owner retained me to sell his company. When we discussed possible buyers, he named one company that he demanded be struck from the list. Given that this buyer was much larger, active in the marketplace, deep-pocketed, and had reason to acquire this seller's company, I asked the owner to explain.

He had two strongly held convictions. First, the owner knew that this buyer paid for its acquisitions only in shares of stock. Second, the buyer's

CEO cheated at golf. While I respected this owner's wishes and pursued other buyers, this buyer fit our target buyer profile so well that I decided to test the owner's beliefs.

Within a few weeks I played golf with the "cheating CEO." During the round, I learned that this gentleman did not cheat at golf. While playing casual rounds like ours, he did take free lifts out of the rough, but only after asking if I minded and only when there was no bet on the hole. I also learned that this CEO had recently changed his company's acquisition policy from paying for acquisitions in stock to paying for acquisitions in cash.

Had I let this owner's beliefs about this CEO and his company color his judgment, we would never have sold this company to the "forbidden buyer" for top dollar.

Buyers entering into negotiations as a cover for collecting competitive intelligence are a rare phenomenon, but it does happen. It is your investment banker's job to protect you from these unscrupulous buyers.

In my practice, we protect sellers by releasing information to buyers in carefully considered and measured doses. We continually test the buyers' intent and sincerity, often requiring them to spend money and meet tight deadlines in order to stay involved in the transaction. As we release increasingly sensitive data to the buyers, we may require them to agree to financial penalties if they fail to close.

Most important, we watch the buyers' behavior. Are they continuing to commit additional funds to the process, and are they meeting deadlines? If they are, perhaps the seller's paranoia is misplaced. Of course, we routinely remove sensitive information from documents (such as customer names or gross margin data) and use creative ways for buyers to access the information they need without jeopardizing the seller's confidentiality (such as allowing a buyer to use a third party to interview the seller's customers). Still, if something just doesn't feel right, we can create a specific and separate nondisclosure agreement (NDA) for a particular document or set of documents.

Constantly, but less formally, before we release any document to buyers we think about how we can prove that they received the information. We imagine the buyers testifying that they couldn't have used the information at issue because they didn't know it. For this reason, my firm uses elaborate systems to ensure that we can prove buyers have received exactly what we have provided them. For a more complete discussion of confidentiality, please see Chapter 10.

The Due Diligence Beast

Let's consider the current weight and heft of the due diligence beast. I urge you to review the Legal and Financial Due Diligence List and the Management System Due Diligence List (Appendix B and Appendix C, respectively). Until early 2010 we did not see lists of this size in the middle-market range. At about that time we entered a buyers' market, and buyers began to take advantage of their leverage to ask for more complex and larger-than-ever amounts of data.

During the boom days of the M&A cycle (2004–2007), buyers were in a frenzy to close deals. Many failed to think about, much less carefully analyze, economic cycles or predict integration issues. As a result, many big buyers were burned at least once, and some were burned quite severely. With that not-so-distant experience in the back of buyers' minds, sellers who are lucky enough to attract buyers without their own battle scars should expect that they will be quite familiar with one or more stories of "good deals gone bad."

Another fuel feeding the growth of the due diligence beast is the new economic reality for law firms. As companies bring more legal work in-house, use contract employees for specific projects, or employ sophisticated software to sort and analyze mountains of documents, law firms now operate in a contracting and highly competitive environment. While many have responded by reducing the number of new hires and steadily lowering salaries for new associates, firms demand more and more billable hours from those associates. (According to the Yale Law School Career Development Office, the demand for billable hours ranges from 1,700 to 2,300 hours per year.) What better project to amass billable hours than to create new and more complex requests for due diligence documents? More altruistically, attorneys can (and do) argue that their increasingly complex due diligence requests are designed to help their clients avoid "bad deals" and, ultimately, save their clients more than they spend.

Law firms aren't the only professionals at the due diligence table. Buyers use accounting firms to request, review, and analyze all of a seller's financial documents. (See Appendix B for a list of financial documents.) But the newest players in the due diligence game are management consulting firms. Buyers retain these experts to analyze all the operational data of a company. Under the operations umbrella, we find human resources (recruitment, training, benefits, overtime hours, etc.), customer retention and warranties, supplier/vendor selection, contracts and rebates, sales and marketing, manufacturing capabilities, shipping, pricing strategies, market surveys, and environmental issues.

For all these reasons, today, sellers negotiate with buyers who accept nothing at face value and who have legions of motivated experts to help them turn over and look under every rock. Today, buyers often demand documentation to the invoice level and are willing to pay handsomely for the assurance doing so offers.

In a recent $15 million transaction, I estimate that the buyer paid at least $500,000 to its team of due diligence experts. While that dollar amount may give you an idea of the scope of the due diligence project, consider also the firepower of the buyer's representatives. Its due diligence team was made up of a Big Four accounting firm, a Wall Street management consulting firm, and one of the biggest law firms in the country.

With players of that caliber across the table, we do everything possible—before starting the sale process—to ready a seller's company and prepare its owners for an extensive due diligence process.

The buyer's cost for conducting due diligence illustrates how buyers also incur expense if they fail to close a transaction. Buyers often part with significant amounts of cash to pay the fees of their high-power due diligence teams. This level of financial commitment can indicate a buyer's seriousness of purpose and may mean that it is less likely to walk from the deal. This may be small consolation to the harried seller on the receiving end of these due diligence lists, but if sellers step back a bit to see the big picture, there is some comfort in negotiating with a buyer who comes to the table having spent money to get there.

If this description of the due diligence beast does not keep you up at night, consider one additional recent development.

You, Too, Can Help Launch Your Buyer!

Armed with leverage and a battalion of experts, buyers' due diligence requests no longer simply reflect the buyers' need for documentation. With greater frequency, we see buyer requests that indicate a desire to involve sellers in launching the new enterprises. Buyers are asking sellers to lend their expertise to integrating the two enterprises or initiating the process by which the buyer intends to make more money than the seller ever did.

In one buyer's attempt to pick a seller's brain about how it (the buyer) could make more money, the buyer made the following request: "Estimate the equipment costs necessary to start manufacturing in-house those products that are currently outsourced."

While you might be tempted to categorize this request as over the top, first realize that to buyers there are no over-the-top requests. In their minds, everything they do during due diligence is designed to minimize risk. Second, in making this request, the buyer has offered us an insight into its post-closing strategy. This buyer is looking for ways to combine its manufacturing capability with the seller's or thinks it can, through this acquisition, reduce its overhead. That's a critical piece of information that an investment banker can use to resist a buyer's efforts to gain concessions from the seller.

In other transactions, a buyer may seek to reduce duplicate personnel expense, so it will likely ask detailed questions about people in management positions, their experience, duties, strengths, salaries, and benefits.

The key question here is how do we navigate the very thin line between reasonable requests—those that reflect what a buyer *needs to know*—and less-than-reasonable requests—those that reflect what a buyer *wants to know*. If you work with a skilled investment banker, he or she should be able to distinguish between the two types of requests. We'll talk more about this distinction in Chapter 9.

THE CASE FOR PRESALE DUE DILIGENCE

If the arguments on the last few pages about the emotional side of due diligence haven't already convinced you of the value of presale due diligence, let me make my case for its measurable benefits. As a nonnegotiable part of the Proactive Sale Strategy, I guide my clients through this dress rehearsal for due diligence for several reasons:

- ◆ Before entering the marketplace, I want to know if the seller's company harbors any outright deal killers or deal cripplers that will lead to seller concessions.
- ◆ Collecting and organizing the data a buyer will ask for in advance of the sale process saves the seller time during the process. Once the sale process begins, time favors the buyer, and I want to minimize the buyer's advantage.
- ◆ In addition to minimizing the risk of not closing and maximizing sale price, the presale due diligence process provides a great opportunity for both me and the owner to see how the other operates.

Deal Cripplers and Killers

Deal killers are issues that make your company unsaleable. Deal cripplers make it unsaleable at its maximum price. Killers can be the process you've used for years to account for inventory or your company's dependency on a single or unstable customer. A killer might be one significant environmental issue or your company's participation in a wounded industry. (As I write this book, the home-building industry comes to mind.)

Some of these killers might be downgraded to cripplers if we can negotiate adequate safeguards for the buyer. Buyers generally equate "adequate safeguards" with significantly lower purchase prices, but occasionally (depending on the nature of the deal crippler) buyers demand other concessions, including that more cash be put into escrow.

Seller Concessions

At this point, let's pause for a moment to talk about the types of concessions buyers demand in their quest for certainty about the quality of their acquisitions. Using the due diligence process, buyers solicit every possible morsel or chunk of information that they believe will minimize their risk in buying companies they know little about. Sellers want to protect information and get maximum prices for their companies. Between these two positions is a great deal of room for negotiation.

So let's assume that, through due diligence, a buyer learns that your company is dependent upon three major customers for 75 percent of its sales. Is this issue a deal killer (end of the transaction), is it a deal crippler (reason for the buyer to reduce its offer), or can it be handled so that the buyer stays at the negotiating table with the same offer? In this case (and many others like it), my task is to assuage the buyer's fears using several negotiating tools.

First, to manage a buyer's concerns, we might negotiate a form of deferred payment: a promissory note (held by the seller), an earnout, or some sort of royalty. Depending on the circumstances (the needs of both seller and buyer and the issue at hand), we may agree to convert a part of the purchase price from cash to a promissory note—guaranteed or unguaranteed—payable to the seller as certain conditions are met. The conditions of the note and all of its terms (payments, dates, interest rate, etc.) are negotiable as well.

Second, we could construct earnouts that are payments that a buyer makes to a seller if the company meets predetermined performance goals after the closing. Generally, earnouts relate to certain sales or profit levels and are used when the seller predicts (but hasn't yet experienced) relatively new or significant growth.

Third, we might choose to use royalties to give a buyer more confidence in the seller's estimates of the company's future performance. If a seller's profit and loss statements do not clearly or satisfactorily illustrate to a buyer how it makes its profits, a buyer may prefer to pay the seller a royalty on each widget it sells after closing than to dissect each line of the seller's P&L.

Finally, we might offer to put a negotiated portion of the purchase price into an escrow account held by a neutral third party (usually a bank). We would negotiate each term of the escrow agreement until we reached an agreement both seller and buyer judge to be fair and reasonable.

Each technique (deferred payments, earnouts, royalties, and escrow agreements) is simply a tool we use to bridge the gap between the seller's desire for a fair purchase price and the buyer's desire to get what it paid for. And each tool is subject to extensive negotiation between the two parties.

When we give an owner a range of possible purchase prices early in the Proactive Sale Strategy, the owner decides whether or not to pursue a sale. During the due diligence process, the owner again decides whether and how to comply with the buyer's requests for information. While many owners expect that the sale process will be difficult, if not impossible, to control, understand that, with a cool head and the assistance of a skilled investment banker, you can retain control of the transaction.

Time Favors the Buyer

Another transaction truism is that time favors buyers. The more time sellers give buyers to perform due diligence, the more time they'll gladly take, the more documents they'll request, and the more issues they are likely to uncover. In conducting presale due diligence, not only do we collect and organize many of the documents that the buyer will request, but we have an opportunity to address the issues that we uncover. For example, if agreements with vendors or customers are not up-to-date, we can fix that. If a lease does not allow a buyer to assume the lease, we may be able to renegotiate new terms. If key employees haven't signed employment agreements or covenants not to compete (if applicable and enforceable in the seller's state), we can see that those are created and signed.

If sellers wait to perform these tasks (and many others like them) until due diligence begins, the process slows to a snail's pace. It helps to recall that the buyer's due diligence process does not commence until the terms of the sale (including purchase price) are set and that purchase prices are upward inelastic. No buyers increase their offers based on what they find in due diligence, but many, many buyers reduce their offers.

Retrading

So many buyers use the data they uncover during due diligence to reduce the purchase price that we have a name for the process: *retrading*. Operating under this strategy, buyers use their high-powered magnifying glasses to locate as many issues as they can that, they contend, reduce the value of the company. Typically, the buyer says something along these lines: "This is so, so unfortunate, but we just discovered that your biggest customer doesn't tie his shoes correctly." (Okay, I admit that this is an exaggeration—but not a large one.)

After emphasizing how distressed they are to learn of this devastating flaw, they reassure the seller that because they are such good guys they are willing to stay in the deal, but they (regretfully) are forced to reduce either their purchase offer or the amount of cash they'll pay at closing (allocating more to postclosing earnouts). From this moment on, buyers opportunistically chip away at the purchase price and secure better terms from owners who have already dreamed about how they'll use the original purchase price.

Here's how one owner faced a buyer who engaged in aggressive retrading.

> Siegfried Applebaum owned a midsize fruit and vegetable processing plant in South Carolina. He'd inherited the business from his father, but his sons had left the business for careers in opera and sports, so Siegfried decided to sell.
>
> Siegfried and his investment banker had engaged as a buyer one of the country's largest frozen and canned food producers. The buyer's representatives had tendered a letter of intent offering Siegfried five times EBITDA for his $2 million company. One week after happily accepting this offer, Siegfried's stop-shop agreement took effect as the buyer dove into the due diligence process.
>
> And that's when the phone calls started. The first had to do with Siegfried's contracts with his growers. The buyer decided that because they were "too loose" it would pay x percent of the purchase price as an

earnout payable to the seller one harvest after closing—if the growers continued to work with the new owner.

The second call came from the buyer's accountants: Unfortunately, they'd discovered that Siegfried's company's financials were not in compliance with GAAP (generally accepted accounting principles). They had restated Siegfried's company's earnings according to GAAP, and the newly calculated earnings were significantly lower than those Applebaum's accountants had provided. Of course, the buyer would "correspondingly adjust" its purchase price.

The next call was related to Siegfried's three key employees: Without employment contracts and covenants not to compete, the buyer couldn't be assured that these three would stay with the company once it took the reins. The buyer was willing to stick with the adjusted purchase price, and, rather than walk from the deal, it would settle for allotting another percentage of the purchase price to an earnout payable to Siegfried one year and two years after closing—assuming, of course, that the key employees stayed with the new company.

Siegfried's investment banker was in over his head. Had he done his research, he would have known that this retrading tactic was a favorite of the chlorophyll colossus. Since he hadn't conducted presale due diligence, he had allowed a buyer to take his client by surprise and had lost considerable negotiating leverage. In the end, these avoidable mistakes cost Siegfried a third of his purchase price.

Sellers should expect every experienced buyer to set the stage for retrading. But before you think that if you reach the closing table without a reduction in purchase price, you have won the war, let's talk about a strategy buyers use to reduce the price *after* closing.

Postclosing Adjustments

Before negotiations begin, some buyers set up price reduction strategies that kick in only after closing. In order to fly under the seller's radar, a buyer must understand the seller's financials better than the seller does. It is not rare or unusual for buyers to outsmart sellers in this way.

A buyer who plans to execute a postclosing adjustment strategy will enter the transaction with a highball offer in its expression of interest, or even in its letter of intent (LOI), confident that it can recoup the portion of its purchase offer that exceeds what it wanted to pay.

Let's look at how one buyer used a postclosing adjustment strategy against a seller.

> Sandy Simms owned a chain of three popular barbecue restaurants with an EBITDA of $1 million. One day an intermediary representing a well-known hospitality group expressed interest in buying all three locations and asked to see Sandy's financials. Two weeks after their first meeting, the buyer sent Sandy an expression of interest offering four times EBITDA (an attractive multiple in the restaurant business), and Sandy was confident she could get full value for her life's work. She pursued negotiations without the guidance of an investment banker and without paying much attention to the last phrase in the buyer's offer, "Four times EBITDA as defined by GAAP (generally accepted accounting procedures)."
>
> What Sandy didn't know, but the buyer did, was that her company's EBITDA was not $1 million but, rather, $500,000. After closing, the buyer successfully argued that Sandy's EBITDA was $500,000, and, in the end, Sandy received the promised four multiple but only on $500,000 instead of on $1 million. Had Sandy known that she'd end up with "half a slab," she never would have entered negotiations.

In another common postclosing adjustment strategy, buyers who understand that sellers' earnings are overstated insert language into the definitive purchase agreement that can be, and often is, overlooked. The hidden land mine reads something like this: "If during the postclosing adjustment period the Company's earnings fall short of Seller's representations, Seller will pay Buyer $5 for every $1 of degradation."

Is it hard to believe that a buyer would have the chutzpah to attempt to slip this kind of language by a seller? It happens all the time. Professional buyers know that even attorneys don't always read the fine print carefully. When buyers plan to use this or any postclosing adjustment strategy, they often employ Big Four accounting firms so that there is no question about the CPA's credibility. They know that few sellers have Big Four accounting firms in their corners.

In either postclosing adjustment strategy, the buyer knows more than the seller about the seller's business and lies in wait until after closing to take its pound of flesh. When retrading, buyers rely on the stop-shop agreements that prevent sellers from negotiating with other buyers for the leverage they need to begin whittling away at the price. When this happens, the seller's only means to halt the downward purchase price spiral is to withdraw from the deal entirely.

An experienced investment banker can help sellers to avoid or limit the impact of stop-shop agreements. (See Chapter 10 for a more complete discussion of these agreements.) If a seller's company is in high demand, the investment banker may negotiate a stop-shop out of the deal completely. But in most transactions, buyers demand—and receive—stop-shops so the investment banker must limit the seller's vulnerability. While there are a number of ways to do so, perhaps the most effective technique is to insert a number of carefully placed hurdles into the agreement. These hurdles can take the form of a date by which a task must be accomplished or additional funds that the buyer must commit to the transaction.

The most rigorous hurdle states that if the buyer attempts to change the terms outlined it its letter of intent, the stop-shop agreement ceases to exist. This strategy is effective, however, only if the buyer believes that there are other buyers at the table. If the seller has not retained an investment banker, buyers know that there are no other buyers.

More common hurdles are those that hold the buyer's performance to a schedule. For example, once the stop-shop agreement becomes effective, the buyer has three weeks to draft its definitive purchase agreement. Three weeks after that date, it must provide to the seller a financing commitment letter, and, three weeks after that, it agrees to have completed, or to waive, due diligence. Motivated buyers do not want to miss these dates if they think they are competing against other buyers.

Again, use your investment banker to help you navigate the stop-shop agreement, but also to steer clear of the common, completely legal, and (in the M&A world) ethical retrading strategies.

A Preview of Behavior

When we work with owners during the presale due diligence part of the Proactive Sale Strategy, we gain important insight into how responsive they are; how they manage numerous, distracting demands; how they maintain objectivity; and, most important, how well they maintain their cool.

If a seller cannot organize the documents required for presale due diligence or the documents are in disarray, we have three options. Option one: If the issues in the documents indicate that this transaction will likely fail to close, I candidly tell the seller exactly that, and we part amicably. In Option two, we dig deeper into the company's records. We bring in the company's CPA to clean up the worst messes so we can begin to anticipate where and how a prospective buyer will attempt to blow holes in the seller's financials.

In a hot M&A market, we have a third option. That is to clean up what we can today, enter the market, and, knowing that the market for this company is active, deal with the issues later in the transaction. If this is the strategy we recommend, we do so only with the full knowledge and consent of the owner.

From the sellers' perspective, presale due diligence offers them the opportunity to evaluate how organized and creative I am (and my firm is), the quality of my associates, the issues I handle and those I ask associates to handle, and, most important, how I prioritize and separate the wheat from the chaff. While we cannot predict with 100 percent certainty exactly what will be important to a specific buyer on a particular day, we can (based on years of experience and significant research into a buyer's motives and deal-making history) distinguish among those issues that will prevent a closing, those that will reduce a purchase price, and those that can be neutralized.

I strongly encourage you to work with an investment banker who knows how to read between the lines of a buyer's due diligence list to understand what plans the buyer may have for the company and what it perceives as its greatest areas of risk. Remember our discussion about buyers using due diligence to involve the sellers (and their expertise) in launching the new venture? Well, a good investment banker has a wealth of experience in distinguishing among those issues that will derail a transaction, those that will cause the buyer to reduce its purchase offer, and those that can be neutralized or managed. There are no transaction truisms that govern the thin and ever-changing line between each type of issue and the others, so sellers are dependent upon the expertise and negotiating abilities of their investment bankers.

Taming the Due Diligence Beast

Presale due diligence is the best way to:

1. Identify and address a company's problems before buyers take the opportunity to use those problems to gain concessions from the seller.
2. Introduce potential sellers to the much more rigorous process they will undergo once a buyer is engaged.

3. Maintain deal momentum in favor of the seller once the transaction process begins.
4. Remove some of the heat from a process that, for most sellers, is emotionally fraught with misunderstanding. Sellers who understand why buyers request the information they do are better prepared to survive the process, arrive at the closing table, and take home a maximum amount of cash (rather than sit waiting for the new owner to pay earnouts based on performance under its ownership).

We take sellers through the presale due diligence process *before* we proceed to step three of the Proactive Sale Strategy: identifying and preparing buyers.

Prescription for Sanity

Appendix B and Appendix C are two generic due diligence lists; the first is a hybrid of legal, financial, and tax matters, and the second covers management issues. If you haven't done so already, I encourage you to take a look at each and—as difficult as it may be—continue to breathe normally as you do so. Keep in mind:

1. These lists are generic. A professional buyer will ask you these questions *and more* related specifically to companies in your industry.
2. There are no "as is" sales. Buyers don't buy companies as is, and yours is no exception.
3. As a rule of thumb, a buyer who is purchasing the stock of your company will be more thorough in its due diligence than a buyer acquiring only assets. But that's only a rule of thumb.
4. Every item and every clause of every item on a due diligence list is negotiable. It is critically important to hire an investment banker, an accounting firm, and a law firm that know how to clear away the unnecessary clutter and negotiate paths through this maze of requests.
5. If you hire the right advisers, you are not helpless in the face of these due diligence requests. Skilled investment bankers are experts in the art of how to disclose and when to disclose information.

4

Step Three: Identify the Competitive Advantage

T he central premise of this book is that it is possible to sell an ordinary company for an Outrageous Price. Let's quickly review what we mean by *ordinary company* and *Outrageous Price*.

Ordinary Company

First, there's no set value to an ordinary midsize company: It may be at the bottom of the scale ($10 million) or near the top ($250 million). For our purposes, the ordinary company is privately held but has no particular management structure. It can be co-owned, family owned, or sole owned. Ordinary companies do not attract infusions of venture capital and do not have patents pending on a cure for cancer or a miracle diet pill. Ordinary companies operate in any industry but generally are in industries that are treading water rather than growing rapidly (e.g., the high-tech sector). Finally, ordinary companies are *saleable,* meaning that they possess sufficient characteristics to attract a buyer willing to pay the average industry multiple.

Outrageous Price

This part is simple: An Outrageous Price is at least two times the prevailing average industry multiple. To achieve an Outrageous Price, we use a two-phase process. The Proactive Sale Strategy (part one) minimizes the chances that the transaction will fail and maximizes the sale price, and is the foundation for part two, the Outrageous Price Process. The Outrageous Price Process is the method we use to leverage a competitive advantage so that (1) if a buyer acquires it, the acquisition creates significant gain or (2) if a buyer chooses not to acquire the company with the competitive advantage, the buyer will experience significant pain . . . enough to motivate that buyer to purchase the company to avoid the pain.

COMPETITIVE ADVANTAGE DOES DOUBLE DUTY

In this chapter, we look at identifying a company's competitive advantage through two prisms: First, doing so is a step in the Proactive Sale Strategy, and, second, the presence of a competitive advantage is a fundamental requirement of the Outrageous Price Process.

Identifying a company's one, or more, competitive advantages early in the Proactive Sale Strategy is critical because understanding the competitive advantage(s) supports the asking price. This understanding gives the transaction adviser—who knows how to use it—a compelling story to tell potential buyers. It also gives buyers assurance that they're getting good value for their money, and it helps owners to focus their energy and attention on what makes their companies valuable. Sellers must know what sets their companies apart from their competitors *before* taking a company to market. In my opinion, the transaction adviser who goes to market without that information does the seller a profound disservice.

In the context of the Outrageous Price Process, we consider the competitive advantage to be the first of Four Pillars of the process. As a sneak preview, the Four Pillars are:

1. A competitive advantage that can be leveraged to persuade a buyer to pay top dollar
2. At least one deep-pocketed buyer active in the marketplace who is motivated to buy because of its desire to eliminate the pain a seller causes it or to exploit the gain a seller offers
3. A seller suited to go the distance
4. An adviser who knows how to execute the Outrageous Price Process

In Part Two of this book, we describe these pillars and devote entire chapters to buyers, sellers, and advisers. But because the competitive advantage is common to both the Proactive Sale Strategy and the Outrageous Price Process, we jump into that discussion here and refer to this chapter as necessary in the second part of this book.

THE HISTORY OF COMPETITIVE ADVANTAGE

A competitive advantage is the feature (or features) that enables a company to make a product or offer a service either *better or more cheaply* than its competitors—*over time.* In the context of the Proactive Sale Strategy, however, we are looking for an existing, or potential, fit between the seller's competitive advantage and the buyer's need. Better yet—and absolutely critical to getting an Outrageous Price for your company—we are looking for a way that the seller's company (1) can (or could, if given time and preparation) meet a buyer's immediate need or (2) could pose a significant threat to a buyer.

In 1980, Michael E. Porter, a Harvard University professor, wrote *Competitive Strategy: Techniques for Analyzing Industries and Competitors* and further investigated the topic in his 1985 book, *Competitive Advantage: Creating and Sustaining Superior Performance.* While Porter did not coin the term *competitive advantage,* he did inject it into the parlance of students in every business school in the United States. All newly minted MBAs recognize the term, and some have a passing knowledge of Porter's method of identifying one's own or another's competitive advantage.

In Porter's world, the reason to identify and nurture competitive advantage is to not only maintain, but also improve a company's financial performance in its daily operations. "Competitive advantage grows fundamentally out of value a firm is able to create for its buyers that exceeds the firm's cost of creating it. Value is what buyers are willing to pay, and superior value stems from offering lower prices than competitors for equivalent benefits or providing unique benefits that more than offset a higher price. There are two basic types of competitive advantage: cost leadership and differentiation." (Porter, *Competitive Advantage*, p. 3).

As an investment banker, I use the concept of competitive advantage not to improve a company's profits (although if an owner is years away from a sale, we will do that), but as a tool to build maximum sale price.

If you wish to dive into the subject of competitive advantage more deeply, I suggest that you pick up copies of Professor Porter's books.

WHAT IS A COMPETITIVE ADVANTAGE?

For our purposes here (understanding how to sell a business for an Outrageous Price), let's use a simple definition of *competitive advantage*: A company's competitive advantage is the product it makes or service it offers either better or more cheaply—over time—than its competitors.

There are three important components to this definition: differentiation, lower cost, and sustainability over time. The first two are exclusive: Your company may do something differently than its competitors *or* it may do or make something more cheaply. Differentiation or cost leadership must be paired, however, with sustainability. To be valuable to a buyer, the ability to differentiate itself or make something (or provide a service) more cheaply *must be sustainable over time.*

Before we focus our attention on how one or more competitive advantages cause a buyer to pay a maximum or even Outrageous Price for an ordinary company, let's look at the issues that make a company fundamentally saleable.

Remember, not all companies are even saleable and therefore will never compete (without much work and planning) for a maximum price, much less an Outrageous Price.

SALEABILITY

I've identified a number of characteristics that buyers look for when shopping for an acquisition. These appear in no particular order, as buyers rank them according to their own needs. As you review this list, consider how you rank—and how a potential buyer might evaluate—each characteristic of your company.

At this point, let's assume that your ordinary company is saleable, but the Million-Dollar Question (or in this case, the Multi-Million-Dollar Question) is: Does your company have a competitive advantage that we can leverage in the Outrageous Price Process?

Table 4-1.

Characteristic	Low Risk	High Risk	Seller's Rank: 1–6 (1 is lowest)	Buyer's Rank: 1–6 (1 is lowest)
Profitability history	Long, profitable history.	Short or unprofitable history.		
Industry segment	Stable or growing. Highly profitable industry.	Erratic or declining growth rate. Generally unprofitable industry.		
Special skill or expertise	No special skill required for success.	Requires highly specialized or scarce skills.		
Location (or lease term)	Location is excellent and can be maintained.	Location is unsuitable and/or requires relocation.		
Relationships	Success is broad-based.	Success depends on limited number of key relationships or customers.		
Labor	Labor is available and relations are good.	Labor is scarce and/or relations are poor.		
Management	Management team is fully qualified, competent, and committed to stay postsale.	Management is unwilling to remain and/or incompetent.		
Return *of* investment	Buyer could liquidate investment for about the same amount as it paid.	Buyer's investment could be easily depleted or is nonliquid.		

Characteristic	Low Risk	High Risk	Seller's Rank: 1–6 (1 is lowest)	Buyer's Rank: 1–6 (1 is lowest)
Return *on* investment	Market, economic, and historical data indicate a continuation of returns.	Without changes in the company, market, or economy, buyer has few prospects for healthy return.		
External factors	Most of the company's requirements for success are within the company's control.	Company success depends heavily on external factors: e.g., interest rates, availability of credit, commodity prices, fashion or style, transportation costs, or foreign sources.		
Reputation	Company is reputable.	Company is unknown or poorly regarded.		
Product/service	High-value, competitive, and responsive to market demand.	Poor quality, overpriced, unresponsive to market demand.		
Regulation	Not subject to special insurance, licenses, franchises, bonds, or governmental regulation.	Subject to hard-to-obtain or expensive insurance, licenses, franchises, bonds, or governmental approval.		
Competition	Limited.	Intense or increasing.		
Technology	Not particularly vulnerable to changes in technology.	Changes in technology have significant and/or negative impact.		
Resaleability	Company could be resold easily.	Company would be impossible to resell.		

DOES YOUR COMPANY HAVE A COMPETITIVE ADVANTAGE?

I don't know, and, if I had to guess, neither do you.

Here's what I do know: Buyers are more likely to pay top dollar for a company that enjoys an advantage over its competitors. These buyers will pay Outrageous Prices only if the company for sale has a competitive advantage that will either eliminate a source of considerable pain or provide a source of considerable gain to the buyer. Chapter 6 discusses how to relieve (or cause) pain or gain to a buyer. For now, let's look at how we go about determining a company's competitive advantage.

I call the process that I use to identify a competitive advantage *hover and dive.* Not terribly technical, I know, but the name gives you a good idea of what's involved in finding the characteristics of a company that we can use to maximize sale price.

The Hover-and-Dive Process

As you may recall, in step one of the Proactive Sale Strategy I ask prospective sellers to answer a number of questions contained in the Sale Readiness Assessment. (See Appendix A for the complete assessment.) These questions cover a broad range of issues (such as an owner's exit goals and relationships with advisers and competitors), but the lion's share is devoted to a company's operations. Operations-related questions include information about pricing, costs, people, sales/communication/marketing, technology, business strategy/business model, industry, customers, and systems.

I use an owner's thoughtful—and usually intuitive rather than fact-based—answers to these questions as the basis for detailed and wide-ranging discussions that can resemble the process a physician uses to reach a conclusion about a patient's complaint, condition, or disease. Based on training, experience, and intuition, physicians start with general questions and then ask increasingly specific questions in an effort to make a diagnosis.

I use the same process as I search for:

1. An understanding of whether this company is saleable
2. The competitive advantage that makes this company unique and saleable at great price

3. Whether the competitive advantage can be leveraged to induce a buyer to pay an Outrageous Price
4. Information that will help me to identify potential buyers

I call this process *hover and dive* because I first hover at a high altitude to get a feel for the terrain. From 2,500 feet, I look for reasons to narrow the focus of my search until I can dive into a possible solution. If a dive does not yield the information I seek (and the first dive rarely does), I return to hover over the terrain, asking questions until I can locate another area that might hold the answer to my question: What does this company create or do differently than its competitors?

Like a physician, my role is to ask insightful questions but also to listen carefully to an owner's intuitive answers. Like a therapist, I ask general questions, but when I hear something interesting I encourage the owner to "tell me more about that." Unlike most investment bankers, I engage in this process because I don't assume that I know all the answers. Each company is unique, as is each owner and each transaction. While there are some patterns common to most, the variation of companies, owners, and paths to the closing table is endless.

Know-It-Alls

As the "patients" in this process, owners answer my questions to the best of their knowledge, but most draw heavily upon their intuition. If an owner can accurately answer every single question that I ask as I hover and dive, looking for the competitive advantage, it raises new questions about the competency and role of the owner's management team. The first question is "Does this business owner, who knows all the answers, hold all of the information between his ears?," followed quickly by "Is this owner's management team really managing anything?" Buyers understand that once the everything-between-the-ears owner exits, profits, if not the entire company, will likely collapse. For that reason, buyers are simply not interested in owner-centered companies.

Intuition: Fact or Fiction?

As I mentioned, most owners draw heavily upon intuition in response to my hover-and-dive questioning. Doing so is completely acceptable, but I must probe further to determine if an intuitive response is a fact or an untested theory. I am reminded of the owner of a frozen food company who, like most owners, answered my questions intuitively. This company's most profitable product was frozen pizza, so I asked him why customers bought from his company. He quickly responded, "Because of its price point in the market."

I had asked this question not only to collect information, but also to test the owner. Was his a statement of fact or an assumption? Could I poke a hole in this statement/assumption to get to what really drove consumers to buy his product? And could I prompt him to think about his product in a different way? My follow-up question was "How often do you send reps into retail outlets to assess the prices of all frozen pizzas in the case?" This owner's answer: "Never."

Both of us learned something important from this answer. I learned that the owner might be correct, but without further investigation we really had no idea why consumers were purchasing his pizza. On the flip side, the owner learned that sending representatives into the marketplace to collect some up-to-date data about his competitors might not be a bad idea.

This owner was quite typical in that he did not know exactly why his customers chose his company's service/product. Owners of midmarket companies are generally so focused on getting the product out the door that they don't have a lot of knowledge about their competitors. It isn't surprising, then, that they don't make the connection between their ability to keep competitors out of their marketplace and how that ability might influence the price a buyer would be willing to pay.

Know-Nothings

I recall meeting with the owners of a North American manufacturer of circuit boards. The company's annual profit was around $20 million, and it managed to manufacture its product in the United States, both characteristics especially valuable to a European or Asian buyer.

When I asked these owners what made their company different, or why customers purchased from their company, they answered, "We have no idea."

The company's expenses were similar to those of its competitors in the industry, but after about five hours of hovering and diving around various topics, I learned that the chief of operations and vice president of sales had instilled a discipline to replace less profitable sales with more profitable ones. They turned away existing or potential business that did not meet a set minimum gross profit margin.

In addition to setting this standard, the managers stuck to it. In two years, these managers replaced $100 million worth of business. They sought out and brought on board customers willing to pay a higher price because the company focused all of its efforts on meeting their specific needs.

This company had differentiated itself from its competitors based on a policy choice its management team had made about a trade-off between sales volume and profitability. This company's management made a conscious decision to serve only its most profitable customers. The team's willingness to turn away less profitable business cut into its volume, but its discipline in adhering to its choice to outperform its competitors in satisfying highly profitable customers and market this distinction to customers willing to pay the higher price created its competitive advantage.

Once we identified this competitive advantage, the question was: Could we show a prospective buyer how to maintain a customer base with these margins? If so, we held in our hands an important key to selling this company for top dollar.

The purpose of hover and dive is to find and make the connection between two dots:

1. What does a company do differently (or more cheaply) than its competitors to make it profitable?
2. Can that activity be sustained over time—even by a new owner?

The questions I ask in hover and dive are intuitive but are also based on objective research, my synthesis of best practices gleaned from hundreds of business books, and my experiences with start-ups and running my own companies. My experience as an investment banker who has orchestrated the sale and purchase of numerous companies for Outrageous Prices also plays a huge role in how I conduct the process.

To me, making connections between what a company does (or could do) to distinguish itself from its competitors and how we might use that characteristic to entice a buyer to pay an Outrageous Price is like moving puzzle pieces until I can see the design. In this process of analyzing and linking information in new ways, I can create a theory (and then a fact-based compelling story) about why a buyer would benefit from purchasing a company. In some cases, linking helps me to see how to show a buyer how *not buying* a company will cause it significant pain.

Let's look at how several sellers (all based on real-life clients) found one or more competitive advantages to leverage into Outrageous Prices. For now, we'll simply take a snapshot of what we learned through the first portion of hover and dive. In Chapter 6 we'll look at how we spun the straw of competitive advantage into the gold of an Outrageous Price.

Clearly Buster's business had several (albeit limited) competitive advantages: economies of scale and location. In addition, Buster had gained valuable experience in favorably affecting legislative action. What Buster didn't have was a *sustainable* competitive advantage, and his business was in a dying industry. These two factors did not make his company unsaleable, but they eliminated the possibility that he could sell it for an Outrageous Price.

DIFFERENTIATION THROUGH SERVICE PROCEDURES AND PERSONNEL

Ignatius Eberhardt owned Wisconsin Medical Waste (WMW), a highly successful company, for almost ten years before he got the itch to sell. Iggy started WMW after noticing, during one of his father's long hospital stays, that the hospital's needle disposal containers were constantly overflowing. He decided that he'd start a medical waste company that would replace the disposable containers with reusable ones that his employees would exchange when the containers were half-full.

Wisconsin Medical Waste outfitted its field technicians in crisp, clean uniforms and operated the cleanest fleet of trucks in the business. Iggy hired a former customer service manager from a five-star hotel chain to train all employees in customer relations.

Ignatius's unique knack for extraordinary customer service helped him gain access to Milwaukee's (and then Wisconsin's) network of hospitals, medical schools, and private medical practices.

WMW quickly expanded its customer base from health institutions to medical and dental offices, nursing homes, and clinics. Iggy added hospital red bag (nonsharp medical waste) to WMW's pickup routes. The company grew steadily and profitably, eventually saturating its market and driving out all competitors but one. Ignatius held at bay this one competitor (the largest in the industry) by providing his customers with meticulous service. If he had to clean up a customer's biohazard room so it reflected WMW's standards, Iggy did so. Not surprisingly, in its ten-year history WMW never lost a customer.

DIFFERENTIATION THROUGH KNOWLEDGE AND BACKWARD VERTICAL INTEGRATION

Green Streets was a New Hampshire–based road builder. It was run by its second generation of owners and had grown under that leadership from $3 million to more than $100 million in revenue.

In addition to building roads throughout New England, Green Streets had carved out a place for itself as an approved contractor to the National Park Service. Although it was not the National Park Service's exclusive road builder in Acadia National Park, it was the preferred contractor.

The engineers at Green Streets had developed methods to adhere to the Park Service's strict requirements in road building. For example, Green Streets successfully built roads without moving any dirt more than 100 feet from its original location. Sensitive to the Park Service's environmental concerns, Green Streets inspected (and if necessary repaired) its trucks on a daily basis to prevent any leakage of oil or other fluids.

Green Streets enjoyed one more—significant—advantage over its competitors: It was the only road builder in the Granite State to own its own quarry. It could control its primary input source (gravel) better than most, if not all, of its regional competitors.

LOWER COST THROUGH DIFFERENCE IN AUTOMATION

Saint Louis Post (a fictional name for a real company) used railroad rails in its production of heavy-duty steel signposts for sale primarily to state highway departments. Its forty-six-year-old owner, Terry, had purchased the company ten years prior to our first meeting about planning his exit from his company.

When we first met, Saint Louis Post was running about $2 million in sales each year, but Terry had lost his mill (which had refabricated rails into bar stock) through eminent domain, leaving him dependent upon competitors for the bar stock needed to fabricate the signposts.

Always a tinkerer, Terry responded to this challenge by developing just one machine (at a cost of about $1 million) to make signposts for $600 per ton. At the time, a division of a major multinational corporation that we'll call "Goliath" controlled 90 percent of the market, selling posts at $1,700 per ton.

Terry had already approached Goliath to gauge its interest in buying him out. Not surprisingly, Goliath could not be bothered.

As I probed Terry's exit objectives, I learned that he would happily leave his company if he could get $5 million for it. Terry had achieved a significant advantage over Goliath and all his competitors through reconfiguring his value chain: making a significant capital investment in creating a different, more efficient, and less labor-dependent production process. His value chain was quite different from his competitors'.

But could we create a strategy to attract this buyer's attention? And did Terry have what it takes to pursue the Outrageous Price? We'll answer those questions in Chapter 6.

LOW-COST LEADERSHIP THROUGH CONTROL OF ONE OR MORE COST DRIVERS

Buster Mann owned Big Man Cig, a low-cost outlet selling cigarettes and beer along the Missouri side of the border with Illinois.

Buster started small: two or three shops. His intent was to put as many shops on the border as he could, so each was a no-frills establishment. Each shop was open twenty-four hours per day and had a drive-through window.

Buster quickly established himself in the best locations, but competitors soon followed. He built as many outlets as possible in the shortest period of time, while his competitors followed suit.

When I met with Buster during an initial, no-commitment meeting, we had to look a little deeper to find Big Man Cig's competitive advantage. Buster had maintained a lead over his competitors, but not a significant one, in the number of locations (economy of scale). The value of the advantage of being first (timing) had eroded over time, and his current locations were only slightly better located and maintained than those of his competitors. With these advantages, Buster could get a fair price in the market, but could he get a maximum, or even an Outrageous, price?

Several months before we met, the Missouri legislature had targeted the tax on cigarettes as a means of raising additional tax dollars. According to Buster, a tax increase (to match those in neighboring states) would "suck the life out of my business, one puff at a time." Buster spent almost a million dollars lobbying members of the legislature and sponsoring ads comparing his cause to that of the Boston Tea Party patriots. It worked. The legislature backed down, and Buster's business continued to grow.

WHAT IS YOUR COMPANY'S COMPETITIVE ADVANTAGE?

At this point, you may think you have a good idea of your company's competitive advantage. In my experience, few owners do have a fact-based grasp on their competitive advantages. Many have a gut feeling for why their customers buy from them, and they do everything they can to maintain or enhance that reason, but few can express that reason in a sentence or even a paragraph. Too busy running successful companies, owners just do not have time to examine each element of their success.

Taking that time is important if you want to sell your company for its best possible price, but it is absolutely critical if you plan to engage in the Outrageous Price Process. In the Outrageous Price Process, not only must you know what your company's competitive advantage is; you must understand which buyer it will attract and how to use that competitive advantage to create pain or gain for that buyer. In Buster's case, we could not leverage a competitive advantage that was not sustainable, or attract a large, deep-pocketed buyer to a business in a dying industry.

So how do you uncover your company's competitive advantage?

A Google search of *competitive advantage consultants* yields several million names and firms. I believe that if you intend to sell your business for a maximum price or Outrageous Price, you must find an investment banker who knows not only how to identify competitive advantage but also how to leverage it fully in the M&A market. As you interview candidates for this position, spend time probing their understanding of this important topic.

5

Step Four:
Identify Potential Buyers

At this point in the process we turn our attention outward to potential buyers in the marketplace. Having completed steps one, two, and three (the Sales Readiness Assessment, presale due diligence, and identifying the competitive advantage), we know if the owner and company are prepared for sale and what makes the company tick. It is now appropriate to identify those companies in the M&A marketplace that can use their significantly greater resources (such as access to capital, more efficient processes, deeper or wider distribution channels, or massive sales force) to make more money from the company for sale than can its current owner.

All investment bankers can provide sellers with lists of prospective buyers. Most firms do a generic search using purchased databases to create those lists. To succeed, both the Proactive Sale Strategy and the Outrageous Price Process require a more refined approach. We spend a great deal of time to conduct a huge amount of research into prospective buyers. While we do have access to several databases, we have created and maintain our own with more than current names of firms actively seeking acquisitions.

We refine that list by determining if there's a credible match between what our seller has to offer and what a buyer might seek. In my experience, the effort we expend in identifying a greater number of qualified buyers is well worth the payoff: a significantly reduced risk of not closing.

TYPES OF BUYERS

There are two primary types of buyers who purchase companies in the $10 million to $250 million range: financial buyers and strategic buyers.

Financial buyers use a financial formula—usually based on a desired rate of return—to determine the price they pay for companies. A private equity group (PEG) pursuing an acquisition for any other reason than to add on to an existing platform is the classic example of a financial buyer. Financial buyers often buy companies in industries they've not been in before, so sellers spend more time (and effort) educating financial buyers. These buyers typically also require more time to perform due diligence because they are learning about the industry as they learn about the seller's company.

A strategic buyer bases its purchase offer on its perception of future value: how well it expects the target company to perform under its management, or how successful the acquisition will be once it can take full advantage of the buyer's better market distribution, name recognition, or proprietary technology.

When a PEG makes an acquisition to add on to existing holdings, it behaves more like a strategic buyer. It pays a purchase price based on its perception of how the acquisition will develop or improve something it is already doing.

There are four types of strategic buyers: competitors, verticals, industry players, and adjacencies.

The first, competitors, is obvious. We look to see if one or more of a selling company's competitors would benefit from acquiring the seller. Competitors usually seek to increase market share and/or eliminate a competitor. Before we add a competitor to the potential buyer list, however, we calculate the risk associated with dealing with a competitor. Not only do competitors know all about the seller's industry, but they can be dangerous when armed with the knowledge that a competitor is for sale.

We also look for potential buyers up and down a company's supply chain. Would one of its suppliers or one of its customers benefit from purchasing the company? If your company is a major customer of one of its suppliers, that supplier may be interested in securing the business of its major customer. It may wish to tighten the link between itself and the ultimate consumer. On the other hand, a seller's major customer may wish to manage its costs by purchasing its source for a critical or costly component.

Industry players are businesses engaged in the same activity as a selling company, but they are not in direct competition with it. For example, an information technology consulting firm in Boston that wants to expand into Atlanta (the home of its most lucrative account) may be interested in acquiring an agency there. Industry buyers are sometimes willing to pay a premium for synergies that include expanding geographic reach, acquiring additional customers, or eliminating overhead.

Less obvious (and therefore requiring more extensive research) are adjacencies. Adjacencies are those businesses that complement the selling company. For example, an electrical supply company may be interested in acquiring a plumbing supply company to expand both its customer base and its product offerings. Unlike competitors, adjacencies do not know as much about the seller's industry, nor are they as dangerous.

Identifying buyers is critically important whether you sell your company using the Outrageous Price Process or via a traditional sale. If you hope to sell your company for an Outrageous Price, however, you will focus your efforts on attracting the attention of a strategic buyer and persuading it to pay handsomely for future value. We talk more about attracting a buyer's attention in Chapter 7.

GAUGE BUYER ACTIVITY

Most owners have some idea about how active the marketplace is for companies in their industries or of their size. But because sales in the midsize marketplace are not publicly disclosed, owners don't know if the active buyers are strategic or financial, what the purchase prices are, or what terms control the deals. Your investment banker should be able to collect much of this data using public sources (such as a company's IRS Schedule K-1s, press releases, and annual reports) and private sources. Most investment bankers also subscribe to various databases that provide information about purchases of privately held companies.

Keep in mind, however, that even those databases do not reveal details about transactions between privately held companies. The databases enable investment bankers to better gauge activity levels, but they must gather competitive intelligence to find the most valuable nuggets of information.

GATHER INTELLIGENCE

Once we have compiled a list of buyers that could benefit most from acquiring a company, we begin to gather competitive intelligence about each. We are digging for details regarding:

◆ Past acquisitions
◆ Prices paid
◆ Changes in their strategic acquisition plans
◆ Problems they may be encountering in their industries
◆ Changes in their industry position or reputation
◆ Personnel changes
◆ Changes in their regulatory environment

To gather competitive intelligence, we turn to a number of sources. We already mentioned the public sources: a company's website, its K-1s, annual reports, and press releases. We scour trade journals for articles and analysis related to potential buyers. Once we've identified the transactions that a buyer has completed in the past, we'll dissect each to determine the motives for the acquisition. What synergies was the buyer seeking, or did it make the acquisition to solve a problem?

We also talk to the prospective buyer's sales representatives about the company's direction, challenges, opportunities, goals, and problems. We ask reps what they know about competitors' actions or plans, and, if applicable, we ask for their opinion regarding what their employer could do to enhance its profitability. While not standard operating procedure, we have asked sales representatives if they think purchasing a company that could enhance profitability is an idea worth pursuing. Sometimes planting just one seed yields a bountiful harvest when a sales rep makes a suggestion to the home office.

Next we ask similar questions of a buyer's M&A representatives. It is not at all unusual for us to talk to various M&A representatives several times each year in an effort to understand what kinds of companies they are looking to acquire.

In short, we do everything we can—without disclosing a seller's identity—to get as much information as possible about one or more prospective buyers before we position our sellers to enter the marketplace. The information we gather helps us to highlight the compelling benefits that we will communicate when we take the company to market.

Buyer Engagement

Gathering information about buyer preferences and behavior is part of our marketability analysis for every company. Before we can predict whether a company is saleable or not or give a seller our best estimate of a purchase price, we must identify and understand potential buyers. If we determine that a company is a candidate for an Outrageous Price, however, we spend a great deal of time focusing on potential buyers.

Remember that to seek the Outrageous Price, we need more than just a list of qualified, active buyers. An Outrageous Price requires that:

1. The selling company has the ability to cause a strategic buyer pain or offer the buyer an opportunity for tremendous gain.
2. The targeted buyer must be highly motivated to relieve that pain or exploit that gain.
3. The seller has both the perseverance to ride the transaction roller coaster and the acting ability to convincingly maintain an attitude of indifference regarding the consummation of the transaction.
4. The investment banker knows how to craft a strategy that makes that buyer understand the value in the acquisition and can inject awareness of the seller's company into the consciousness of the selected buyer.

All of these pillars of an Outrageous Sale are discussed in Part Two of this book.

Even before taking a company to market, an investment banker can actively, yet anonymously, engage a prospective buyer. Through a series of contacts, a transaction intermediary can glean more specific details about what a particular buyer typically pays for companies in the seller's industry, who its negotiators are, what attributes it looks for, and what problems it commonly encounters. With all of that information in hand, when a seller announces its intent to sell, it does so with all its ducks in a row.

Let's turn our attention to the behavior you can expect from buyers during acquisitions.

WHAT TO EXPECT FROM BUYERS

Over the years in working both with buyers and across the table from them, I've observed several important characteristics that often control or influence their behavior. I share those observations here because the more you know about buyers (and their motives), the better prepared you are to get from them what you want.

Buyerspeak

Buyerspeak is the name I give to the devastatingly effective weapon that buyers use to undermine a seller's confidence and thus reduce the seller's resistance to a lower offer for the company. To engage in it, a buyer carefully chooses a "front person" to connect with, impress, and inflate the ego of the seller. Before making any offer, the front person deliberately says and does everything he or she can to deflate the seller's opinion of the company's value. All sophisticated buyers are fluent in buyerspeak, but not all sellers know it when they hear it. If you aren't familiar with it, your investment banker should be able to recognize it for what it is and thus neutralize its effect on you.

With "pay as little as possible" as their mantra, buyer representatives use this language because it works. The words they use and their style of delivering those words are carefully designed to:

◆ Undermine sellers' confidence in the value of their companies
◆ Undermine sellers' confidence in their advisers—especially in the adviser negotiating the sale for them
◆ Make sellers grateful for the offer a buyer ultimately makes

Buyers pull tried-and-true favorites from their "buyerspeak phrasebooks" such as: "Ultimately, we don't care whether we do this deal or not" or "We always talk to employees before we make an offer" or "These are the standard documents that we use in every deal." Whenever a buyer says "always" or "never," warning bells should sound in your head.

In addition to the phrases common to nearly every deal, some buyerspeak is tailored to specific situations, such as: "We only pay a four multiple for companies like yours" or "You don't need an investment banker. They cost you time and money." Really? Ask any buyer if it uses investment bankers, and the answer is always yes.

There's no way to alert you to every example of buyerspeak because buyers spend hours in their conference rooms figuring out exactly what they can say or do to shake your confidence in your asking price. Your best defense is to understand that buyers orchestrate the very first, the very last, and every single contact with sellers to achieve one and only one goal: to pay the least amount possible for a company.

In the buyer's conference room bets are made on the spread: How much of your purchase price can it chisel away by taking money back in postclosing adjustments or through claims against your representations and warranties? (See Chapter 3 for a discussion of postclosing adjustments.)

If I've made it seem as if you are swimming in a sea of sharks, you are. In Chapter 10 we'll talk about all the characteristics you should look for in an investment banker, but this is a good time to suggest that you look for one who knows how sharks think and how they hunt.

Buyers Put the Cart Before the Horse

We've established how buyers think: They say and do anything to lower a purchase price. But how do they do it? Buyerspeak is one example. Another is to make requests of a seller that, if granted, demonstrate weakness on the seller's part. For example, buyers may ask to visit the seller's plant *before* they make an offer. They may ask to meet with the seller's employees or banker. If a seller grants any one of these requests—many naïve sellers do so even *before* prequalifying the seller's ability to pay—the buyer has drawn first blood, and it will thirst for more.

What's the Rest of the Story?

Buyers are experts at collecting information, but they never share it. For example, you will never hear a buyer tell a seller how it expects to eliminate half of the seller's overhead or that its accountants have uncovered a fatal flaw in the seller's financial records. Keeping information like this from sellers has a profound (and costly) effect on a seller's payday.

The investment banker you want to hire knows how to figure out what the buyer isn't saying. I've already admitted that investment bankers can't read minds, so how can they uncover what the buyer isn't sharing? First, the investment banker should spend time analyzing your company—inside and out—to find its competitive advantage (see Chapter 4). Second, the investment banker must do a great deal of research to uncover any synergies between your company and the buyer's. Third, he or she must make a hypothesis about what the buyer has up its sleeve and then create ways to test that hypothesis. Basically, I'm suggesting that the best way to uncover a buyer's hidden agenda is to engage in the Proactive Sale Strategy whether or not you intend to go after the Outrageous Price.

The Proactive Sale Strategy reduces a seller's risk of failing to close the deal, but it also increases the seller's chances for getting the sale price he or she wants—even in a tough M&A market. It does so by carefully preparing the seller's company, aligning the seller's assets to the buyer's needs, and understanding and acting upon the buyer's priorities and preferences.

PART
2

The Outrageous Price Process

6

The Four Pillars of Selling Your Business for an Outrageous Price

Let's turn now to the much more intriguing question and the subject of this book: Is your company one that could sell at a price more than two times what the average financial buyer would pay? Or, in other words, *can your company sell for an Outrageous Price?*

Again, before you dismiss the possibility, I ask you to consider the value your company might have to a buyer who would experience tremendous gain or relief from pain by acquiring it.

Before you answer, let me offer a metaphor for the very real intangibles present in the Outrageous Price Process.

If I were to unearth from my musty basement a small forgotten painting passed down through generations of my family, I might estimate its "garage sale" value based on the size of the canvas and the appeal of the subject matter. If I notice that the painter's name is Vincent van Gogh, I quickly call an expert, whose estimate of value includes far more factors than the physical characteristics of the painting. While that expert knows the value the market has historically paid for this painter, he or she also considers the value to the collector who has spent a lifetime searching for this painting or to the two museums vying for the title "Largest van Gogh Collection."

Estimating a sale price of a "priceless" piece of art to a collector who needs to possess it is much like estimating an Outrageous Price for an ordinary company. We look not only at the physical characteristics of the company, but also at what it offers to the buyer who needs it.

Typical estimates of sale price include not only an analysis of a company's financial statements, but also assumptions about the future performance of the company, the health of the M&A market, and the cost of credit. This information is important; however, it does not indicate how much a company might be worth to a buyer who understands its potential or who could capitalize on synergies between the two. Similarly, standard estimates of sale price don't even begin to predict what your company might be worth to a buyer who would experience tremendous gain or relief from pain by acquiring it.

The Proactive Sale Strategy that I describe in the first part of this book and the carefully orchestrated Outrageous Price Process that I describe in Part Two go far beyond the typical estimate of sale price. While the Proactive Sale Strategy can be used alone to maximize sale price and minimize a seller's risk of failing to close, it can also be used to assess whether a company has the potential to sell for an Outrageous Price. The purpose of the Outrageous Price Process is to extract that Outrageous Price from a buyer.

CAN YOUR COMPANY FETCH AN OUTRAGEOUS PRICE?

Financial buyers use financial formulas to determine the price they will pay for a company. In its most rudimentary form, these buyers establish the minimal rate of return that they require and work backward to a purchase price. An Outrageous Price is one that is at least two times the prevailing average industry multiple of EBITDA (earnings before interest, taxes, depreciation, and amortization). I assume that you are aware (or as aware as you can be) of the multiples for your industry. Imagine, for a moment, being paid twice what those multiples would suggest.

To help determine if your company is a candidate to fetch an Outrageous Price from a strategic buyer (one who does not use a simple formula but instead pays based on its perception of future value), we will look at the analysis and process that enabled some not very remarkable companies to do so.

I do not intend any disrespect in characterizing these companies as less than remarkable. Each was run by an owner driven to achieve excellence, but it is not necessary for *your company* to be extraordinary to sell for an Outrageous Price. As you'll see in Pillar I, it simply must have a competitive advantage that it can leverage.

We describe in detail the four components (or pillars) that support the Outrageous Price. As you read the short introduction to each, keep in mind that all four must be present for your company to have a chance at grabbing the brass ring (an Outrageous Price). The absence of any one extinguishes the prospect of selling for an Outrageous Price but does not mean that the company cannot sell for a *premium* price.

Pillar I: Competitive Advantage

In the Proactive Sale Strategy, we spend time identifying the company's competitive advantage. If a company does not have a competitive advantage, we cannot initiate an Outrageous Price Process. If a company has a competitive advantage, we can investigate the possibility of engaging in the Outrageous Price Process. Our first question is: Can the competitive advantage be leveraged to entice a buyer to pay an Outrageous Price? Can we use that competitive advantage to show a buyer how acquiring the company would spare the buyer a great deal of pain or yield tremendous gain? These are the key issues as we seek to sell a company for an Outrageous Price.

In Chapter 4, we discussed the hover-and-dive process that we use to determine why a customer chooses one company over its competitors.

In the Outrageous Price Process, competitive advantage is the foundation for determining either (1) how the selling company causes a potential buyer pain or (2) how that company offers a potential buyer considerable gain. Once we make that determination, we work to create a strategy to persuade that buyer to pay a price commensurate with the amount of relief or gain it achieves through the acquisition. The price we are seeking is the Outrageous Price (two times the average price prevailing in the marketplace).

Pillar II: Buyers in the Marketplace

In Chapter 5, we talk at length about buyers, but our focus now is on the second pillar of the Outrageous Price Process: buyers who pay Outrageous Prices. Who are they? What do they look for in an acquisition? How do they behave?

In Chapter 8, we look at the characteristics of the Outrageous Buyer and then at the reasons they can be persuaded to pay Outrageous Prices. For a seller to get an Outrageous Price, there need be only one buyer at the table. We'll talk about how to locate the buyer that will pay handsomely to make the acquisition necessary to relieve it from the pain it currently experiences or to reap tremendous gain.

This idea of pain relief or gain is incredibly important to our analysis and to your ability to get an Outrageous Price for your company. Specifically, we ask:

◆ Does your company provide the buyer, through its competitive advantage, a means to achieve outrageous gain? To realize gain, a buyer might need proprietary technology, the right geographic location, particular expertise, a highly successful marketing program, an ace sales organization, or access to a specific marketplace.

◆ Is there a buyer in the marketplace that would prefer to acquire your company (because of the pain it is causing) rather than compete with it? Chapter 7 discusses how to leverage a competitive advantage in a way that helps a buyer conclude that acquisition is a far, far better thing than competition.

Pillar III: You, the Seller

In Chapter 9, we talk about you—the seller. We will determine if you've got what it takes to demand and get an Outrageous Price for your company. As buyers contend (using buyerspeak) that they do not need to purchase your company, you, as a seller, must maintain—and mean—that you do not need to sell your company. Buyers will engage in a carefully orchestrated process to undermine your confidence in your sale plan. We look at the strategies buyers use and how sellers must behave if they are to succeed in getting the Outrageous Price.

Pillar IV: Advisers

In Chapter 10, we look at the type of transaction adviser you need to help you through the process I've developed to sell your company for an Outrageous Price. We discuss exactly what characteristics a transaction adviser needs to possess to orchestrate an Outrageous Sale.

ARE THE PILLARS IN PLACE?

If your company has the "right stuff," you've got some decisions to make. Can you leverage your company's strengths to relieve pain or create tremendous gain for a buyer? Are you the type of person who can stay the course? Can you find experienced advisers to steer the transaction to an Outrageous Closing? To go for the Outrageous Price, you need patience and an ability to perform under pressure. Your adviser needs all that and experience, creativity, good instincts, and serious negotiating skills. The two of you must trust each other completely. If you've got what it takes, I believe, as do the owners I've represented, that the rewards are worth every bit of the hard work.

If, however, you suspect that, because one of the Four Pillars of an Outrageous Price is missing, your company is not a candidate for an Outrageous Price, do not despair. You join approximately 90 percent of owners who want—and receive—top dollar for their companies. Chapter 11 describes the technique—the competitive auction—that we use to achieve that goal and talks about how the competitive auction works, the role you play in it, and how to avoid its major pitfalls.

7

Pillar I: Leverage Your Company's Competitive Advantage

$\mathbf{I}$f we were evaluating your company's ability to sell for an Outrageous Price, at this point we would have already identified your company's competitive advantage and identified one possible buyer for your company. It would now be time to determine if there is a link between what your company has to offer (its competitive advantage) and what the buying company might gain or the pain it might alleviate through acquiring it.

To justify paying an Outrageous Price, a buyer must benefit in one of two ways: The buyer must either (1) anticipate tremendous gain from its purchase or (2) desire significant relief from the pain that the selling company is causing it.

Does your company's competitive advantage provide a buyer a means to achieve outrageous gain? Can a buyer leverage your company's propriety technology, advantageous geographic location, particular expertise, highly successful marketing program, crack sales organization, high-quality customer list, or access to a specific marketplace?

Or can you and your investment banker persuade a buyer that acquiring your company is so preferable to competing with it that it will pay an Outrageous Price to eliminate your company as a competitor?

To create the environment necessary to persuade a buyer to pay an Outrageous Price, your investment banker must link what your company offers to what a buyer wants, and that link must be quantifiable.

Your investment banker must create a financial model that clearly demonstrates to a potential buyer—in quantifiable terms—the financial benefit it will experience from purchasing your company. For example, if your company could successfully roll out a number of subsidiaries in a competitor's backyard, your investment banker must convincingly predict the dollar effect your actions would have on that competitor's earnings.

Keep in mind that a potential buyer's initial response to your investment banker's theoretical model will likely fall somewhere between shock and cynical amusement. The former response usually indicates that the buyer has never considered your company to be capable of posing a credible threat (or offering considerable gain). The latter comes from buyers who are already working to undermine your confidence in your ability to sell for top dollar.

As you will see in the case studies that follow, a buyer's initial reaction is not as important as how that buyer behaves once we quantify the value of the seller's company in the buyer's hands (for example, in terms of cost reductions or additional sales).

I recently represented a medical supply company (EBITDA = $1 million) that provided consumable medical products to ambulance companies. The seller had identified the best buyer and hired me to conduct a traditional competitive auction that would bring this buyer to the table and push the purchase price as high as possible. I suggested that this owner consider pursuing an Outrageous Price because:

◆ The seller's company had a competitive advantage in its regional control over the ambulance service market.

◆ There was a large buyer active in the marketplace.

◆ The seller was willing to walk from the deal if he couldn't secure the price he wanted.

◆ I am an adviser who knows how to orchestrate an Outrageous Price Process.

As I suggested earlier, once we establish that all Four Pillars of the Outrageous Price are in place, we have to ask: Can we leverage this company's competitive advantage to create buyer gain or relieve buyer pain?

In this case, the theoretical or financial model that I used to demonstrate the effect the purchase of the company could have on the buyer was to show how the buyer could absorb the seller's sales and eliminate overhead. Most of the gross profit margin would fall to the buyer's bottom line. In addition, with the seller out of the marketplace, the buyer could increase its prices.

As is the case in most transactions (and in all Outrageous Price Processes), we orchestrated a competitive auction. When we opened the auction, we received offers in the $4 million to $5 million range. Our targeted buyer's bid was in that range. Over the next several months, however, we continued to show our targeted buyer how valuable this acquisition could be. Once this buyer accepted the financial model we created at the beginning of the process, it paid the Outrageous Price: $8 million for a company worth $4 million.

A WORD ABOUT EARNINGS

Before we jump into the pain/gain discussion, let me add one note. When we discuss (in Chapter 11) the sale process that we use to sell companies to third parties, the competitive auction, you will observe that if a selling company's earnings deteriorate during the auction process, the value of the buyer's offers falls. The relationship between a fall in earnings and fall in purchase price is not related to the type of sale process we use. It is, however, related to the type of buyer at the table. If the buyer is a financial buyer, one who bases its offers on financial formulas, those formulas generally include earnings.

In contrast, the investment banker engaged in the Outrageous Price Process works with buyers that base their purchase offers on a perception of future value, not current earnings. In the aforementioned medical supply case study, the company's earnings fell to $0 before closing, yet the buyer still paid an Outrageous Price based on its expectations of the company's future value under its ownership.

CREATING GAIN

One way that a company can create gain for a buyer is in the quality or quantity of the customers that the selling company brings to the buyer.

Creating gain often relates to margins. For example, you may have a contract to sell your company's widgets to Walmart and Lowe's. While your margin is low and your customer base is limited, you have volume on your side. Furthermore, you maintain relationships with powerful retailers that may be invaluable to a potential buyer. Even with low margins, your company could become extremely attractive to a larger company wanting to break into your market.

Conversely, you may have a roster of high-quality customers that are willing to pay a higher price because your company's service (or marketing, technology, patents, etc.) is so outstanding. Your sales are smaller, but your margins are impressive.

We emphasized the ability to create gain when we took the circuit manufacturer from Chapter 4 to market. We were able to sell that company to a Fortune 50 company for millions of dollars more than the prevailing industry multiple.

This company made circuit boards and enjoyed net profit margins of about 10 percent. Its sales staff was able to convince customers that its outstanding customer service was worth the higher price. This company quickly cut loose those customers that did not appreciate the value in superior service. Adhering to a disciplined strategy that is rare in any industry, this company worked with only the best and most loyal customers and did not waste time with those that did not fit its model. The company chose its customers, not the other way around.

Although this company was not the market leader in terms of size or sales, its high-quality client list was coveted by a larger competitor—and eventual buyer. Once at the table, this buyer was anxious to close the deal because it had so much to gain. It raised a minimal number of questions and erected few hurdles, so the deal went through with barely a glitch. (A rarity in any transaction!)

Company reputation and image can also be a competitive advantage. Many large corporations have managed to tarnish their reputations, and the acquisition of smaller, more reputable companies can be gateways to improved relationships. A high-tech company with a spotty history of product launches might purchase a smaller competitor with a perfect product launch record. This buyer might pay handsomely to enhance its reputation in the marketplace and restore customer confidence.

Finally, a buyer's gain is often related to its preference to buy rather than build. It's often easier to buy an existing company than to start one from scratch. Every day deals are made for this reason. As you'll see in the case of Green Streets later in this chapter, a multinational corporation stood to gain a great deal by purchasing a company with a virtual monopoly on road-building services in the northeastern United States. Once a buyer is able to see the potential gain, the sale process becomes very interesting.

EASING PAIN

In Greek mythology, the mother of Achilles, the bravest hero of the Trojan War, dipped Achilles into the magical waters of the River Styx in an attempt to make him immortal. Unfortunately for Achilles, she forgot to dip the heel by which she held him. Because Achilles' heel was untouched by the waters, that small area was mortal and, therefore, vulnerable. The vulnerability we are looking for in an Outrageous Buyer can be just as small and hard to find as Achilles' heel.

While the Achilles story is just a myth, the vulnerability of many companies is not. Companies often have one area of singular weakness, and our mission is to (1) find it and (2) exploit it. More technically, that's known as (1) finding the pain and (2) leveraging the competitive advantage.

The key to creating pain is to find some way of irritating the larger company—whether it's through price margins, public bidding, license agreements, better technology, subcontracts, or any other weakness the other company may have. Ask yourself, "Am I doing something significantly differently or better than this potential buyer?" If the answer is yes, you are on the right track to finding your buyer's vulnerability.

If you don't immediately recognize a potential buyer's weak spot, you are not alone. Owners are often blind to the leverage they can exert against larger competitors or larger companies. Owners are so focused on expertly running their businesses that it often takes an outside third party who knows what he or she is looking for to recognize the buyer's vulnerability.

Almost every company has an Achilles' heel, but it takes creativity and insight to see how your company might leverage its strengths to exploit that vulnerability or create gain for a buyer. Once you've identified your company's ability to relieve pain or create gain, it's time to evaluate whether you and your adviser can leverage that competitive advantage to create gain or alleviate pain.

LEVERAGING COMPETITIVE ADVANTAGE TO CREATE SIGNIFICANT BUYER GAIN

Let's look first at how we go about determining if a competitive advantage has the potential to create significant gain for a buyer.

Recall Green Streets from Chapter 4. It had a competitive advantage based on a differentiation in knowledge and backward vertical integration. This New Hampshire–based road-building company was an approved (and preferred, but not exclusive) contractor to the National Park Service. Over the years, its engineers had designed road-building techniques that adhered to the Park Service's strict requirements in road building. For example, Green Streets successfully built roads without moving any dirt more than 100 feet from its original location. Sensitive to the Park Service's environmental concerns, it inspected (and if necessary repaired) its trucks on a daily basis to prevent any leakage of oil or other fluids.

In addition to its knowledge of and compliance with multiple and often confusing Park Service regulations, Green Streets had, through its own acquisitions, vertically integrated its supply chain. At the time I met with Stewart, its owner, Green Streets owned a quarry in the Granite State, allowing it to control its primary input source better than most, if not all, of its regional competitors.

Green Streets was run by its second generation of owners and had grown under that leadership from $3 million to more than $100 million in annual revenue. Stewart had groomed the management team so well that he was spending no more than fifteen hours per week on company business.

A multinational construction conglomerate had approached Stewart and offered him $38 million for the company. Stewart suspected that his company was worth more and initially asked me to perform a market valuation.

After a review of all the factors, we predicted that we could sell Green Streets for 3.5 times its EBITDA, so we estimated that Green Streets would be worth $50 million in the marketplace. Stewart agreed that $50 million better reflected his idea of the company's value and decided to pursue that price through a competitive auction.

Readers who recall the Four Pillars of an Outrageous Price may be wondering: "Why not go for the Outrageous Price? You've got a company with several competitive advantages; a huge buyer active in the marketplace and already interested in the seller's company; a seller who does not need to sell, at least not immediately; and an investment banker who knows how to orchestrate an Outrageous Price Process!"

That's all true, but at the time I met Stewart, I hadn't yet formulated the Outrageous Price Process. While I had observed that similar companies sold for wildly divergent prices, I hadn't figured out why. I assumed that sometimes owners got lucky or sometimes buyers paid too much or sometimes the market just overheated. In this case, we didn't intentionally go for the Outrageous Price. Instead, we deliberately set up a competitive auction to make sure Stewart would get top dollar—from whatever buyer stepped up to the plate.

Once I put Stewart's company on the market, the multinational company increased its bid to $43 million. Other bids came in around $50 million, and a few private equity groups pushed the bidding into the $60 million to $70 million range. Stewart's value expectations were confirmed in the place where it counts: the marketplace. Real buyers thought Stewart's company was worth far more than $38 million.

As the auction progressed, the strategic buyers at the table (those not basing their bids on financial formulas) moved ahead of the financial buyers. I spoke with each bidder—including the multinational bidder—answering questions and showing each how Green Streets could offer it huge potential gain.

First, in acquiring Green Streets, a buyer could gain access to current and future National Park Service contracts. Not only did Green Streets know how to bid successfully for contracts; it enjoyed a stellar reputation for completing them as promised.

In the case of the multinational bidder, we learned that it had already purchased large road builders in the southeastern United States, but that it hadn't been able to find a toehold in the Northeast. To successfully expand into the mid-Atlantic states, this multinational did not want to compete with Green Streets—a formidable adversary.

During this period of time, government funding for highway construction was increasing dramatically, and Green Streets was uniquely poised to exploit this opportunity.

Finally, there was the quarry. Unlike most of its competitors, Green Streets controlled the price of one of its most significant input costs.

We communicated frequently with this multinational buyer about all the ways it would benefit from acquiring Green Streets. When it understood our case, it offered $85 million, and Stewart agreed that we'd found our best offer. (An offer I would later call the *Outrageous Price.*)

LEVERAGING COMPETITIVE ADVANTAGE TO RELIEVE BUYER PAIN

In addition to leveraging a competitive advantage to create significant gain, there are many ways to alleviate pain for a potential buyer. In Chapter 4, we introduced Terry, the owner of Saint Louis Post. Terry had created a machine that produced signposts much more cheaply than the process its giant competitor, Goliath, used. This chapter discusses how we demonstrated to Goliath that it was less painful to pay Terry an Outrageous Price than to have its prices undercut in a public bid situation.

As you'll see, it took only a Mother's Day, a Father's Day, and an owner's birthday sale to give Goliath a headache big enough to scramble for its checkbook. Once we found Goliath's vulnerability, we exploited it and sent shock waves through its normally stable marketplace. Goliath paid an Outrageous Price to eliminate Saint Louis Post from its marketplace and secure its owner's commitment not to compete.

Pain: Case Study #1

Terry's company, Saint Louis Post, had a significant competitive advantage based on cost leadership gained through a difference in automation. As you may recall, the mill that Saint Louis Post had used for refabricating railroad rails into bar stock necessary to create heavy-duty steel signposts closed (due to eminent domain). Terry responded to this loss by developing one machine, at a cost of about $1 million, to make signposts for $600 per ton.

You may also recall that Terry's largest competitor, a division of a major multinational corporation that we'll call Goliath, controlled 90 percent of the market and was selling posts at $1,700 per ton.

When Terry and I first met, Saint Louis Post had about $2 million in annual sales, and Terry told me that he had already approached Goliath to gauge its interest in buying him out. Not surprisingly, Goliath was not interested. The market share that Goliath would gain through purchasing Saint Louis Post was not significant enough to make an offer, much less an offer of an Outrageous Price. During our meeting I also learned that Terry would happily leave his company if he could get $5 million for it.

One pillar of the Outrageous Price Strategy was in place: Saint Louis Post clearly had a competitive advantage, but could we leverage it? At first glance, Pillar II seemed to be in place as well: a large buyer in the marketplace. But could we persuade it to pay twice the industry's average multiple? Pillar III is an owner/seller who can trust the process, trust his or her investment banker, and stay on script. Could Terry maintain an "I don't need to sell" attitude? Pillar IV is the investment banker who knows how to pull all the pieces together and go for the Outrageous Price. Terry had come to the right place.

We'll talk in detail about the other three pillars in subsequent chapters, but let me digress just long enough to point out once again that even with all the pillars seemingly in place, there is no guarantee that the four ingredients will lead inevitably to an Outrageous Price. We know that the Outrageous Price is not possible if one pillar is absent, but even with all four present the process is still subject to all of the unpredictabilities of human and corporate behavior.

Knowing that (1) Terry had a significant cost advantage over Goliath and all his competitors, (2) there was a large buyer in the marketplace, and (3) Terry was willing to trust the process, we decided to go for the Outrageous Price.

Our theory was that the best way to leverage Terry's competitive advantage was to cause our targeted buyer pain. Terry and I used the public bidding process that states use to purchase highway signs to catch Goliath's attention. As an experiment, we chose a small state and submitted our bid to provide signposts at $900 per ton.

Within days Terry got the reaction we were hoping (and had planned) for—the call from our targeted buyer. "What are you doing to our market?" he asked. "What you are doing will screw both of us!"

Terry answered truthfully, "This bid won't screw me. I can sell as low as $600 a ton and still make a profit."

Graciously, Terry invited Goliath's representatives to visit his plant. Goliath could not resist the chance to see what Terry was doing to undercut its price.

Terry and I carefully staged the visit. I drove Goliath's representatives by a bank Terry partially owned and on whose board Terry sat. I casually mentioned Terry's other holdings. When we arrived, Terry's plant was clean and well organized. We scripted everything to show Goliath that Terry had deep pockets, that he wouldn't be driven out, and that he certainly had the capacity to hurt Goliath's post-making division.

Once in the plant, the visitors were visibly impressed that Terry's machine required only one guy to run it compared with Goliath's reliance on union-heavy shops. That signaled to them Terry's ability to undercut Goliath indefinitely.

As we neared the end of the visit, one of Goliath's representatives asked if Terry's company was for sale. I answered that Terry would consider a sale only if the price was based on his company's future value and the profit it would generate for its buyer. Terry would not entertain any discussions of a price based on current sales or EBITDA. Predictably, Goliath ignored us and left town.

Soon after, Saint Louis Post held a Mother's Day sale offering signposts at a significant discount. Goliath's people called us to express interest in buying Terry's company. In June of that same year, Terry held a Father's Day sale. At this point, Goliath's customers started calling to ask why Goliath had charged them so much over the years when Saint Louis Post wasn't charging nearly as much. These calls increased Goliath's willingness to negotiate.

Only when we were ready did I communicate to Goliath Terry's asking price of $20 million. Not surprisingly, Goliath hung up the phone. I suggested that Terry celebrate his birthday with a birthday sale, selling posts priced at an even greater discount.

Meanwhile, I had been looking into the probability that several potential Chinese buyers could pose a threat to Goliath if they had Terry's technology. As my investigation proceeded, I learned that, while the Chinese buyers might pose a threat to Goliath, they were so wedded to their financial formulas that they'd never pay the Outrageous Price we were seeking. Their presence in the marketplace, however, contributed to the leverage we were able to exert against Goliath.

Within days of Terry's birthday sale, Goliath called me with an offer of $7 million. Price negotiations stretched out over several months until Goliath offered Terry $14 million for his $2 million company.

As part of the negotiations, I asked Goliath about an employment agreement for Terry. I admit I did not anticipate its response. Instead of an employment agreement, Goliath was interested only in a noncompete agreement for Terry. We had assumed that Goliath wanted Terry's expertise and his machine. Instead, Goliath wanted the patent on the machine and Terry banished from the marketplace.

Terry signed Goliath's noncompete, the deal closed, and Goliath promptly destroyed Terry's machine, dismantled the plant, and sold the real estate. More significantly, within a year it raised the price of steel signposts from $1,700 per ton to $2,400 per ton.

Through the purchase, Goliath now controlled the marketplace. Goliath had not been motivated by gain: Taking its market share from 90 to 100 percent would not have caused it to pay an Outrageous Price. Eliminating a competitor that had demonstrated its ability and willingness to disrupt the market brought Goliath to the table and made it willing to pay an Outrageous Price.

Pain Case Study #2

In Chapter 4, we also met Ignatius Eberhardt and his company, Wisconsin Medical Waste (WMW). WMW had a lock on Milwaukee's medical waste market. Iggy had spent years cultivating relationships with customers and upgrading the company's services. WMW's trucks were cleaned daily, its representatives made their rounds in clean white uniforms, and employees were trained in customer service by a manager who had worked for a five-star hotel chain. Most critical to its customers, WMW organized such frequent pickups that a medical sharps container never reached capacity, much less overflowed.

I didn't know all this when Iggy decided to sell. In fact, I hadn't even met him. Like many owners, Iggy decided that he could negotiate directly with the most logical buyer, National Medical, a huge firm that controlled 85 percent of the national market. Iggy had successfully kept National Medical out of the Milwaukee market for years. His gift for creating extraordinary customer service helped WMW gain access to the city's network of powerhouse hospitals and private medical practices.

Iggy and National Medical eventually struck a deal for $6 million, or four times EBITDA—a standard multiple in the medical waste industry. After months of contentious negotiations, National Medical failed to show up on closing day. The deal fell through, and Iggy's plans to climb the highest mountain on each of the seven continents crumbled.

Iggy resumed running his highly successful business but had newfound energy to keep National Medical locked out of the Milwaukee market. When National attempted to build a new disposal facility in Milwaukee a year or two following the failed negotiations, Iggy used his considerable political connections to close the facility for environmental reasons.

Eighteen months later, Iggy blew the dust off his mountain-climbing dream and decided to try once again to sell WMW. This time, he sought my help.

At that point in my career, I had not formalized the Sale Readiness Assessment (see Appendix A). I would ask most of the questions in the assessment, probing the responses that would lead me not only to determining if the owner was ready to sell, but also to what it was that made the company unique. In

Iggy's case, we spent three days in a conference room, decorating the walls with huge lists of ways in which WMW was different from its major competitor.

I started researching potential buyers. We looked at private equity groups, competitors, and those involved in adjacent industries. Iggy wasn't interested in selling to a PEG because he wanted more than the standard multiple for his company. The adjacencies we identified might be interested, and we would eventually use them to create an auction. But of all the possible buyers, National had the most to gain from a purchase of WMW—if we could not only attract its attention, but persuade it to make an offer that exceeded $6 million.

Was the possibility of gain enough to persuade National to return to the negotiating table with a much better offer? Maybe or maybe not. To answer that question, we began to search for National's vulnerability. In this case, what could we do to make *not* buying WMW painful for National? What could be more painful for National than acquiring WMW? We believed that it would be significantly more painful for National if WMW expanded and became a dangerous competitor in other markets, especially in Chicago, where National was headquartered.

We created an expansion plan. At the same time, we drew up detailed five-year projections about what WMW would be worth if our expansion plan succeeded. In five years, we reasoned, WMW would be worth $20 million.

We notified WMW's attorneys and CPAs of our plans. WMW then began applying for permits to do business in the Chicago area. Because the permitting process is public record, National quickly got wind of our applications and called Iggy, demanding to know what WMW was doing.

As we had scripted in advance, Iggy told National that because he was focused on expansion plans, it would have to talk to me, his investment banker. He told National that the experience during their first go-round had taught him that he needed someone else to manage acquisitions while he stayed focused on running the company. Iggy told National that he wasn't interested in selling, but if they wanted to pursue anything related to acquisitions to talk to me.

When I received the first call from National, its representative causally asked if WMW was, indeed, for sale. I told National that Iggy had decided to expand and that we were considering acquiring National's East Coast operation. National's representatives were flabbergasted and assured me that WMW could not buy National's East Coast operation because National was going to buy WMW.

That initial phone call was the first sign from National that our strategy of causing pain in order to elicit a better offer was going to work. Had National not reacted so quickly and with obvious concern, we might have been forced to shift our strategy. But a shift was not necessary.

We commenced a three-month exchange of phone calls, during which I had ample opportunity to politely remind National that it had very little credibility in Iggy's eyes, after backing out of the deal years before. Finally, after courteously but repeatedly informing National that Iggy was too busy planning WMW's expansion to evaluate a sale, I told National that if Iggy were even to consider a sale it would have to make an offer of $20 million, no less. Predictably, National rejected the Outrageous Price, and we rejected all of its lower offers. In the meantime, Iggy continued applying for permits in northern Illinois, southern Wisconsin, and western Indiana, and National grew increasingly nervous.

To achieve my goal of maximizing the chance that a deal will close, I always formulate a backup plan. The backup plan for WMW would increase the pressure on National. During our evaluation of potential buyers, we had identified a multinational company with enough cash to buy WMW that dabbled in the medical waste business. According to our backup plan, we approached the multinational company and secured an offer for $6 million.

Word of the offer (but not the amount) quickly circulated back to National, and the news put pressure on National. Over the next few months, National gradually raised its offer. We rejected each until National made what we considered to be a serious offer: $18 million. Iggy graciously agreed to sell.

One year passed between the day that Iggy retained my firm and his closing date. Three years had passed since National took its $6 million and left Iggy standing at the altar. During those three years, WMW's profits and sales had *not improved*, but National tripled its offer to $18 million.

National was willing to pay an Outrageous Price to avoid the prospect of competing against WMW in markets it was accustomed to controlling. We based our Outrageous Price Process on that assumption, tested it by pulling permits, and it paid off.

Clearly, one of the keys to succeed at securing an Outrageous Price is to create a situation in which it is far easier and preferable for the buyer to purchase your company than to deal with the consequences. That defines finding a company's pain.

THE OUTRAGEOUS BUYER IN THE COMPETITIVE AUCTION

The sale process that we used in all three of these cases—and in all others in which we achieved the Outrageous Price—is a competitive auction. (We describe that process in detail in Chapter 11.) However, there's a twist to the auction when there's an Outrageous Buyer in the mix.

In a competitive auction, we invite all prospective buyers—including the buyer we expect to be our Outrageous Buyer—to submit offers. Remember, identifying an Outrageous Buyer is a prediction based on the best data we can collect. It is not a sure bet.

We invite other buyers to the table in an effort to ensure that (1) we have included any buyer that could (unpredictably) become an Outrageous Buyer and (2) if our predicted Outrageous Buyer is not, for reasons we could not anticipate, excited about the selling company, the seller still reaps the best price the market will offer.

As we conduct the competitive auction, the Outrageous Buyer—either the one that we expected or one we did not—identifies itself through its better-than-its-competitors' offer. While we continue to engage the other prospective buyers and encourage them to increase their offers, we enter into a negotiated sale (one between one buyer and one seller) with the Outrageous Buyer.

We conduct the competitive auction with the non–Outrageous Buyers at the pace that our progress with the Outrageous Buyer dictates. While we carefully plan and conduct all interactions with all buyers, I spend more time with an Outrageous Buyer than I do with others to make sure that the Outrageous Buyer understands how its failure to purchase my client's company will cause it pain or why acquiring it holds vast upside potential. That time is rarely wasted.

If your company has a competitive advantage that we can leverage to create gain or alleviate pain for just one buyer in the marketplace, another piece of the Outrageous Price Process puzzle slides into place.

The next challenge is to figure out how you and your investment banker can demonstrate to that one buyer how much it will benefit from acquiring your company. Can the two of you create a strategy that demonstrates to a buyer—without letting that buyer know that you are actively selling your company—how acquiring your company will yield it outrageous gain? Or can you persuade a buyer (as did Terry and Iggy) that acquiring your company is so preferable to competing with it that it will pay an Outrageous Price to do so?

We begin to answer these questions in the next chapter.

8

Pillar II:
The Outrageous Buyer

As we discovered in Chapter 4, there are hundreds, if not thousands, of ways that a company might distinguish itself from its competitors. Most successful companies do possess at least one advantage, and sometimes more, over their competitors. But having an advantage isn't enough.

CHARACTERISTICS OF AN OUTRAGEOUS BUYER

For an Outrageous Price Process to take place, we need to find a buyer with three critical characteristics.

1. The buyer must have very deep pockets.
2. The buyer must be motivated to eliminate pain or exploit gain.
3. The buyer must have a champion inside the organization pushing to make the deal.

Deep Pockets

Perhaps the most important Outrageous Buyer characteristic is the size of its pockets. The buyer we seek in the Outrageous Price Process does not break a sweat to come up with the purchase price. It does not need a bank or investors to finance the deal, so it need not seek approval for paying an Outrageous Price.

While many companies have deep pockets, we are looking for pockets so deep that the buyer either expects no scrutiny about paying an Outrageous Price or can easily tolerate any resistance. Outrageous Buyers typically have revenues in excess of $1 billion, but, most important, they can make outrageous multi-million-dollar expenditures with ease.

To pay an Outrageous Price, a company must be large enough that the outrageous part of the purchase price is immaterial; an extra $15 million, $20 million, or $25 million is a tiny drop in its huge bucket.

In companies with pockets the size we are discussing here, there is little reason for scrutiny about payments of Outrageous Prices because in annual reports the dollars spent for one acquisition are lumped in with all the acquisitions the buyer makes in a fiscal year. Even shareholders who review their annual reports with a magnifying glass remain blissfully unaware that the company paid a twelve multiple for a smaller company.

It is often in the buyer's best interest to bury the Outrageous Price it pays for your company. In addition to its shareholders, it does not want owners of future acquisition targets to know the multiple it paid for your company, nor does it want to broadcast that price to its past sellers—many of whom may be still working for the bigger company.

Motivated to Eliminate Pain or Maximize Gain

The Outrageous Buyer we seek is one who makes an acquisition based on its expectations either of what it will gain from the transaction or of the transaction's ability to eliminate a persistent pain. By definition, this buyer is not a financial buyer (one who makes purchases based on a financial formula) but a strategic buyer.

In Chapter 7 we looked at several examples of transactions in which buyers paid Outrageous Prices. In the first, we were able to show a buyer how Green Streets (with its competitive advantages as a successful road builder for the National Park Service and owner of a quarry) could yield tremendous gain for the buyer. In the second, a buyer paid an Outrageous Price to eliminate the pain that Wisconsin Medical Waste was causing— and could cause in the future. In a similar third example, a large company purchased a much smaller competitor so it could control the product price in its marketplace.

In all cases, not only did the buyers have very deep pockets, but they were highly motivated to buy because of a desire to eliminate pain or exploit significant potential gain. Each also had one additional characteristic of an outrageous buyer: an internal champion pushing to make the deal.

Internal Champion

There must be one person in the buyer's organization who is invested in purchasing your company and who can effectively make the case that it is worth paying an Outrageous Price to do so.

When we engage in negotiations to sell a privately held company with, for example, $5 million in sales to a behemoth with $20 billion in sales, the CEO of the large company is not involved in the transaction and in all likelihood is not even aware of its existence. Instead, the smaller company has caught the attention of the chief of one of the large company's $100 million divisions. Perhaps the smaller company has demonstrated an ability to damage the profit margins of this division—thus putting the division chief's bonuses, or even job, in jeopardy. Or the smaller company offers something that could create huge gain for this same division—thus leading to sizeable bonuses for this same division chief.

In either case, if the Outrageous Price Process is to succeed, this division chief must have sufficient clout to argue the case for the acquisition to his or her superiors—superiors who must sign off on the purchase price.

How can a seller know if the person with whom we negotiate has the necessary leverage to close the transaction? The investment banker you hire should probe this question as he or she does all others during this process. One way to do so is to listen carefully to the interaction among the buyer's representatives. If the division chief's opinions are neutralized or ignored during telephone or in-person conversations, that person may not be able to close a transaction at an Outrageous Price. If, on the other hand, the division chief's opinions are respected and his or her suggestions are acted upon, another piece of the Outrageous Price puzzle slides into place.

BUYER BEHAVIOR

When we refer to the *buyers* in the Outrageous Price Process, we are referring to the individuals who represent the companies making the acquisitions. These representatives are professionals in the same way that players in the National Football League are professionals: They make their living *exclusively* from negotiating the purchase of companies like yours. This is not a hobby or a onetime thing for them. Buyers are highly educated, and they use that education and years of acquisition experience to support comfortable, if not opulent, lifestyles. The less they pay for your company, the more money they make for themselves and for their employers.

Large corporations employ a host of these buyer representatives, most of whom you will never meet. The one you do meet will have been carefully chosen based on his or her ability to impress and connect with you. Expect the buyer you negotiate with to be of a similar age, share your hobbies and your ethnic group, and be (or pretend to be) of a similar personality type.

Beyond that, the typical buyer has excellent "people skills" and, despite all appearances, has little or no decision-making power. These folks play their parts so expertly that few sellers ever realize they are part of a performance.

Finally, be aware of a factor in every buyer's behavior that is commonly referred to as "winner's curse." You have probably experienced a mild form of winner's curse if you've ever negotiated to buy a big-ticket item (a house, a car, a horse, a boat, etc.). Your challenge is to make an offer that—ever so slightly—exceeds the seller's definition of acceptable.

In an auction situation—especially in an auction for an item with a fluid value, such as a company—buyers often experience a much more virulent form of the curse. In the car, boat, or real estate transaction, buyers can gather enough information about the commodity to make a fairly informed bid. In the acquisition of a company, however, the buyer makes an offer before it has a chance to gather all necessary information. The buyer's uncertainty about whether it is bidding against itself creates additional pressure. Further, the buyer of a company wants its bid to preserve as much profit for itself in the deal as possible. This tension between bidding high enough to win and low enough to preserve profit creates an anxiety that underlies all of a buyer's actions.

PREPARE THE BUYER

Let's assume that your investment banker has identified a potential Outrageous Buyer for your company. (That buyer has deep pockets and is active in the marketplace.) Let's further assume that your company has a competitive advantage that your investment banker believes he or she can leverage to either relieve pain or cause gain to that Outrageous Buyer. Now what?

To reach this point, your investment banker has presumably gathered a great deal of intelligence about this buyer. It is time now to use that information to create a strategy designed to make your company known to the prospective buyer without any hint that your company is for sale. Ideally, we engage the buyer's attention so it makes an offer to purchase before we take your company to market.

If the targeted buyer fails to act first, your shot at an Outrageous Price is not lost. Introducing your company to a potential buyer (in a positive light and without any connection to a sale) *before putting it on the market* can still bear fruit.

CATCHING THE BUYER'S EYE

There are as many strategies to catch a buyer's eye as there are companies. Strategies vary based on the unique strengths of the seller and the particular vulnerabilities or opportunities of a buyer. For that reason, rather than force your company into a cookie-cutter eye-catching strategy, you want to find a creative investment banker who can cook up the right recipe for your company and your prospective buyer.

As an example, allow me to recount a strategy that my firm used with an industrial lighting supply company. Through our research, we identified a large electrical parts company as a prospective buyer. We learned that it had experienced a number of widely publicized recalls on its wire and electrical components primarily designed for the residential construction industry. Over the past few years, it had made several acquisitions in related industries to improve its retail distribution reach but had not been able to crack the industrial lighting market. A tarnished reputation and inexperience in that marketplace had hindered its growth.

We predicted that one way to attract this buyer's attention was to place advertisements in several major publications for players in the home-building industry. These tasteful and professionally developed ads highlighted the awards for product quality that this soon-to-be seller had accumulated over the years.

We supplemented this ad strategy with carefully worded conversations with this buyer's representatives. We also planted the seed with its manufacturer's reps that one way to overcome consumer wariness might be to bring in a subsidiary well known for its adherence to the highest standards of quality.

Two weeks after our first ad appeared, the owner (not yet seller) fielded an inquiry from a representative of our targeted buyer. The owner and I had carefully prepared for this call by scripting his response and practicing variations of the call several times.

If, like this owner, you are seeking the Outrageous Price, your response to a buyer's initial inquiry is a first, but important, step in your overall strategy. For example, in this case, the response that best fit this owner/seller's overall goal was to:

1. Wonder aloud how the buyer's representative could have assumed that his company was for sale (given its strong earnings, solid niche in the marketplace, etc.).
2. Honestly deny that the company was for sale. (He had not yet agreed to sell the company.)
3. Add, as an aside, that the owner's energy was currently so focused on expanding into the residential lighting market that he really didn't have time for the distraction of a sale.
4. Confide that, of course, one day—if the right offer came along—he'd consider a sale.
5. Ask the buyer's representative why the buyer identified his company as a possible acquisition and listen carefully to the response.
6. Warmly thank the buyer's representative for showing interest in his company.

At the conclusion of this call, the owner knew that we had attracted the buyer's interest and had gathered some preliminary (but not necessarily reliable) information about the motives for the buyer's interest, and the buyer understood that this smaller fish was thinking of entering its marketplace. In this particular situation, it was time to implement the next phase of our strategy: Leverage the seller's competitive advantage, which in this case meant competing—quite visibly—with the buyer in its marketplace.

Other situations call for different approaches, but every bid for the Outrageous Price demands that the investment banker craft a response to a buyer's inquiry that opens and furthers the dialogue between buyer and seller and keeps the seller in the driver's seat.

The primary issue at this initial stage is to determine the most opportune moment to introduce the investment banker into the process. If the seller makes that introduction too soon, the buyer knows that the seller is actively pursuing a sale. If, on the other hand, the seller engages the prospective buyer in even the most general conversations about a possible sale without the advice and counsel of a skilled investment banker, the risks to that seller are significant.

Buyers are professionals. Unlike most sellers, they have negotiated numerous transactions and will take as much information—and cash—from a seller as the seller allows. Reread Chapter 5 for a quick refresher on some of the tactics buyers use to gain the upper hand in the buyer–seller relationship.

BUILDING THE BUYER RELATIONSHIP

We've already talked about how buyers generally act in outrageous and traditional transactions. Let's conclude that discussion with some ideas about what you as a seller need to understand about *your particular buyer.*

First, you need to understand why prospective buyers are attracted to your company. If you have engaged in the Proactive Sale Strategy, you have made an excellent start in answering this question. You have identified your company's competitive advantage, considered a wide variety of buyers, and worked to match your company's assets to a prospective buyer's needs.

If you pursue the Outrageous Price Process, the need for understanding why a buyer is at the table goes into overdrive. Because buyers don't share their motives, your investment banker may not know initially why a buyer is interested in your company. As the relationship with the buyer develops, however, uncovering that reason must be one of his or her top priorities. Understanding a buyer's motives is a critical component of the overall Outrageous Price Process that your investment banker creates.

Do you recall the case of Wisconsin Medical Waste in Chapter 6? The ultimate buyer approached the seller with an offer that the seller refused. The seller and I then spent nearly two days going through a process that eventually evolved into the Sale Readiness Assessment. (See Appendix A.) During those two days we put the seller's business under a microscope and gathered and analyzed all the information about the buyer that we could find. Slowly, we were able to make a plausible assumption about why the buyer was interested in this much smaller company. Using that theory, we then determined how the buyer would behave and how we could leverage the seller's competitive advantage. Our theory about the buyer's motives was not one that we could ever confirm, but it was one that we tested repeatedly, and it governed every step we took from the first conversation with the buyer to the closing table.

Understanding a buyer includes recognizing the buyer's alternatives. For example, if you are negotiating to buy a Lexus SUV, you know that for about the same price you could get comparable features in an Acura, BMW, or Mercedes. The Lexus salesperson knows that as well. Similarly, as a seller of a company, it is important that you understand what your buyer's alternatives are. The more comparable alternatives your buyer has, the weaker your negotiating position. The fewer alternatives (the situation in the Outrageous Price Process), the stronger your negotiating position.

Finally, take time to understand incentives of all parties at the table— especially the buyer. In the purchase of a car, a salesperson is keenly interested in whether your spouse *has to have* a Lexus. A company's incentives are never as clearly stated, but if your investment banker has done his or her homework, is a student of human behavior, and has significant experience in dealing with buyers, he or she should be able to pick up cues about a buyer's incentives.

A buyer's incentive typically falls into one of two categories. The buyer's representative is charged with:

1. Acquiring some level of financial performance. *Financial performance* in this case generally means profit.
2. Making an acquisition that solves a specific problem. For example, the buyer identifies acquisition targets that it believes will yield significant synergies. (See the industrial lighting example earlier in this chapter.)

There's one more party at the table: you, the seller. If you engaged in the Proactive Sale Strategy, you spent time assessing your motives for a sale during step one: assessing the owner's and the company's sale readiness. In defining your goals for the transaction and your "ideal" sale, you have gone a long way toward understanding your incentives to sell. If, however, you plan to pursue an Outrageous Price, there are a few other tasks you must accomplish. In the next chapter we'll discuss what it takes for an owner to go for the Outrageous Price

9

Pillar III:
The Outrageous Seller

W e've looked at the competitive advantage or quality that must be present in a company for it to sell at an Outrageous Price, and we've looked at what motivates buyers to pay lots of cash for a company. We've observed how ordinary companies leverage their competitive advantages to persuade much larger companies to pay handsomely to acquire the gain or relieve the pain these competitive advantages cause.

The question now is: Do you have the personality to take the less-traveled road to the Outrageous Price?

First, the good news: If your company enjoys the very competitive advantage that the best deep-pocketed buyer is willing to fork over millions of dollars for, you are halfway there! And now the bad news: In the world of the Outrageous Price, you won't ever see those millions if *you* don't have what it takes to play the Outrageous Price game.

As an owner, pursuing the Outrageous Price requires three personal characteristics: the ability to trust your adviser, self-discipline, and a sizeable amount of acting ability. All three must be present if you are to successfully sell your company for an Outrageous Price. Before you dismiss any or all of these characteristics as either unimportant or unnecessary, let's look at how each fits into the Outrageous Price Process.

TRUST

I place the ability to trust your adviser at the top of the "what it takes" list because it is foundational to the other two. As you'll see, all the self-discipline and acting ability in the world aren't enough if you don't trust your adviser to know what he or she is doing. For a moment, think of getting an Outrageous Price as a military operation. You will be asked to follow orders (often seemingly counterintuitive orders) from a commanding officer. Of course, that takes courage and self-discipline, but underneath it all you've got to trust the judgment and experience of a battle-tested veteran.

Unlike in the military, in the Outrageous Price Process, you choose the person who leads you into battle. If you've done your job well (Chapter 10 contains a complete description of the qualities to seek in an investment banker), the adviser you pick will have the intuition, creativity, judgment, and experience to lead you to the Outrageous Price. And also unlike military service, you, not the commander, hold ultimate power: You can reject or accept any and every offer along the Outrageous Price road.

If you can't trust your adviser enough to leave the driving to him or her (even for just a few months), you can go for the brass ring, but, I assure you, your chances of catching it are nearly nonexistent.

I realize that telling self-reliant, up-by-their-bootstraps entrepreneurs to "let go" and trust their advisers completely is not an easy sell. If you are like most owners I've represented, asking for your complete trust while you ride the wildest emotional roller coaster of your life is a scary prospect. There will be times when you want to take the money—good money—and run for the nearest exit. Only owners with self-discipline, a convincing ability to act, and trust in their advisers have what it takes to walk away from an "average" deal to hold out for the Outrageous Price.

SELF-DISCIPLINE

Going for the Outrageous Price takes all the self-discipline owners can muster—usually in the form of limiting contact with a buyer or remaining patient despite innumerable delays.

You've either got self-discipline or you don't. I've represented owners who have the right company to attract the right buyer, but we don't even attempt to pursue the Outrageous Price. Why? That owner is either too demonstrative or expansive to control him- or herself or too tightly wound to trust anyone to orchestrate the Outrageous Price Process.

Deciding to Sell

Before you decide whether you've got the guts to pursue an Outrageous Price, let's take a moment to look at what's at stake. Selling your business is probably the most important financial transaction of your career. Because you've likely worked many years to build your business, there is *great* emotion attached to letting go of your company. It is likely that either family members work in the business or you've developed close friendships with key employees. Perhaps your standing in the community is tied to your ownership of your company. People implicitly trust or respect you because of the financially stable enterprise you've built.

Most business owners are passionate about their businesses—if they weren't, they wouldn't put in the countless hours that they do. The decision to sell is understandably a difficult one.

As enjoyable as dreaming of retirement is, many owners can never make the leap from owner to retiree. We all know seventy- and eighty-year-old owners who continue to run their businesses knowing full well that their exits are inevitable. These owners offer a myriad of excuses about why they have not yet detached themselves from their companies.

I never try to persuade these—or any—owners to sell their companies. I don't believe there is a one-size-fits-all answer to the question "When is an appropriate time for an owner to sell or to retire?" Only you can determine if you have the energy and good health necessary to run a successful company.

For owners who are simply tired of running the company, it is worth exploring whether there's a way to reconfigure their involvement before jumping to the conclusion that now is the right time to let go. I urge owners to

Gut Check

1. When you have confidential information, you share it with only:
    a. _____ close family members
    b. _____ trusted advisers
    c. _____ close personal friends
    d. _____ those who need to know
    e. _____ other

2. Associates describe you as:
    a. _____ gregarious
    b. _____ a lone ranger
    c. _____ a people person
    d. _____ a planner
    e. _____ other

3. Advisers are:
    a. _____ there to solve a specific problem
    b. _____ to be kept on a short leash
    c. _____ interchangeable
    d. _____ too focused on their task to see the big picture
    e. _____ other

4. I've tried to sell my company:
    a. _____ never
    b. _____ once
    c. _____ several times
    d. _____ other

5. I describe my negotiating skills as:
    a. _____ outstanding
    b. _____ effective
    c. _____ strategic
    d. _____ intimidating when necessary

Answers: There are no correct answers. These questions are ones your adviser will be asking you (explicitly or implicitly) as he or she evaluates your ability to pursue the Outrageous Price.

make a clear-eyed assessment of their goals and of their companies before making the decision to make a business exit.

To help you assess whether you've got the self-discipline to pursue the Outrageous Price, I've created a short questionnaire. I encourage you to think carefully before answering each question as honestly as you can.

In the Outrageous Price Process, sellers have innumerable opportunities to demonstrate their self-discipline. Limiting their contact with the buyer and exercising patience are two of the most common ways sellers demonstrate (or don't) their grip on their emotions.

Limit Contact with the Buyer

Bob Carlson was an affable seventy-year-old business owner from Macon, Georgia. Bob was the consummate salesman and had used that talent to build one of the largest peanut processing plants in the southeastern United States.

Before Bob and I took his company to market, we talked about how buyers would do and say almost anything to undermine Bob's confidence in his asking price and minimize the price they'd pay for his company. Bob assured me that he'd been around the block once or twice, so there was nothing a buyer could say or do to shake his focus.

Not long after purchase negotiations commenced, the buyer started calling Bob's office directly. I intervened, informing the seller to direct any questions to me, but the calls persisted. Bob answered one of these calls and in the course of the conversation said he'd be happy to answer any of the buyer's questions and would show the buyer his plant. Unbeknownst to me, he did just that and introduced the buyer to his key employees.

A week later, the buyer's representative joined Bob in his booth at a regional meeting for peanut farmers. Bob made sure to extract a promise that the buyer would keep quiet and watch. The buyer did indeed watch and then made, in Bob's opinion, some "ungentlemanly" comments. Bob quickly ejected the buyer from the booth and as soon as the show was over called me to tell me about the incident.

There was little I could do to calm Bob because the buyer's representative had already called to tell me that the deal was off. Two weeks later, two of Bob's key employees left the company, and, without their ongoing expertise, there was no way to resurrect that deal or even find another buyer.

> Bob was convinced that the buyer was behind the departure of his key employees—so convinced that over the next two years Bob spent tens of thousands of dollars pursuing a lawsuit against the buyer and his former employees.

In running your business, you are the alpha dog. The important issues reach your desk, and you resolve them. You draw on your experience and instincts and talk to the parties involved. You (like all sellers) lack experience in the Outrageous Price Process, so you must trust the instincts of your investment banker and limit your contact with buyers. Minimizing contact with a buyer gives you tighter control of the strategy you and your investment banker have chosen.

Buyers know investment bankers are much better at sticking to their strategies than are sellers, so they look for ways to probe sellers to find the "chink in the armor." Buyers attempt to catch owners with their guards down and employ a variety of methods to do so. They may call or text you or even "happen to run into you" at your child's baseball game or at church.

To avoid these encounters, don't take phone calls on the fly. Make sure whoever screens your calls knows the identity of each and every caller before you accept the call. Strategies unravel when a receptionist cheerfully tells a buyer, "He's been waiting for your call!" That piece of information is a clear signal to the buyer that the seller was anxiously awaiting the buyer's response and instantly puts the buyer in the driver's seat. Make sure your support team understands the rules of the game.

During scheduled or "chance" meetings with the buyer, you must resist the temptation to give away *any* information. This is easier said than done. Last year, I was sitting in a conference room with my clients and the buyer's team. Up to this point, one of the sellers had been extremely protective of his company's customer lists. When the buyer suggested that it conduct a blind survey to verify how many of the seller's customers were likely to stay with the company once it had been sold, this seller candidly noted, "They won't tell you anything on a survey." Falling back into his role as consensus and relationship builder, he candidly noted, "Let's just go on out and talk to each one of them!" Suffice it to say that we didn't act on his suggestion.

We recommend that sellers have no contact with their buyers, unless the seller and investment banker determine that there is something specific to be gained.

In selling your company, you must step back and let your investment banker do the negotiating. If you've chosen your adviser well, he or she will have the experience and intuition to predict what is going to happen and how best to respond. He or she is far less emotionally involved in the sale process than you are. Savvy buyers will interpret your overtures (phone calls, e-mails, or other communications)—no matter how small or seemingly helpful—as signs of weakness. Don't talk to the buyer unless doing so is part of a preplanned strategy.

If you can't resist leaving your mark on the process, the process may not be for you. At least, consult your adviser before you do anything that might jeopardize your goal: getting the Outrageous Price.

Patience and Deal Fatigue

Do you have the patience to endure a negotiation process (over which you have little control) and allow your carefully crafted strategy take its course? In the National Medical purchase of WMW, there were many times when the seller wanted to take the buyer's money and run straight to the bank. He stayed in the game because he was able to concentrate his energy on the ultimate goal—an Outrageous Price—rather than on the day-to-day, seesaw-like progress of negotiation.

Having patience also means that, no matter how tempting, you don't count your chickens before they are hatched. If you've already spent your sale proceeds in your imagination, you will begin to lose your cool when the deal process gets bumpy. Sellers who talk to friends and family about all the money they are going to make inevitably lose their confidence when the deal shows signs of faltering. They think, "I've lost the dream," and subsequently lose their ability to think rationally. It is not uncommon for deals to fall apart (either permanently or temporarily) at the eleventh hour, so you must maintain your composure until the wire transfer clears. You must convince yourself that selling today to this particular buyer just doesn't matter.

Regardless of whether you pursue the best possible price or the Outrageous Price, all transactions take time to complete. The smoothest transactions take months and run off track more than once. The process wears on everyone—especially on type A business owners who get worked up emotionally and lose patience with the painstaking process of moving the transaction ball inches or, at best, feet instead of yards. That said, sellers who see their transactions through to a successful completion figure out a way to handle the fatigue that is part and parcel of the sale of a company.

In the Outrageous Price Process, sellers are further challenged by the fact that their investment bankers work incrementally to increase the value of the buyer's offer. It's a bit like mining a vein of precious metal. You make sure that the shaft you've created is solid before drilling or blasting farther. As the buyer's offers enter the realm of "outrageous," it is naturally tempting for sellers to accept less than their target price.

Self-disciplined owners can endure months of negotiations. They trust their adviser's judgment enough to be able to approach a huge pot of gold without appearing interested. Further, they can and do walk away from multiple tempting offers to hold out for the Outrageous Price. They are, and you must be, mentally and financially prepared to lose the deal and start all over again if necessary.

Most deals fall apart at least ten times before they close. That's why it's essential to have an adviser who can manage emotions: his or hers, yours, and those of the buyer. Managing emotion is often the difference between closing and not closing the deal.

I remember one transaction that exemplifies the deal fatigue that all sellers experience at some point during the transaction. The buyer was consistently asking the seller for small concessions—none of them deal breakers—but, cumulatively, they began to wear on everyone involved. The seller considered each request carefully, sometimes devoting considerable mental energy to his decision. In each instance, however, the seller refused to concede the point. But with each new request, his angst grew. Finally, on the eve of closing, the buyer made a very minor last-minute request. The seller blew up and called to tell me to walk away from the deal—immediately. He was emotionally drained. Like many sellers, he suffered from deal fatigue.

We coaxed the seller back into reality by sitting down with him in a relaxed setting. I asked him why he was so upset. He replied, "I've given in time and time again. Now they want us to pay the cab fare back to the airport! That's it! I just won't do it." It was only when I pointed out that he had not given in on a single concession that he began to calm down. I helped him realize that he was reacting to the strain and stress of each request from the buyer. As requests piled up—each requiring a decision on his part—his stress level increased.

In reality, this buyer had behaved quite reasonably, continuing to negotiate despite the fact that its requests were repeatedly denied. This seller, like so many others, experienced deal fatigue not as a result of conceding various requests or from having to deal with an unreasonable buyer. He had lost perspective by devoting energy to making a decision on each of many negotiating points.

As Baumeister and Tierney note in their book *Willpower: Rediscovering the Greatest Human Strength,* "The link between willpower and decision making works both ways: Decision making depletes your willpower and once your willpower is depleted, you're less able to make decisions" (p. 98).

Your investment banker may not be able to keep you from becoming fatigued, but he or she should be able to share with you some strategies to limit how severely fatigue affects your ability to make the multiple decisions necessary to achieve your goals. At a minimum, authors Baumeister and Tierney make a strong case for including more low-glycemic foods in your diet and getting more sleep!

ACTING ABILITY

In addition to trust and self-discipline, owners who take home an outrageous amount of money for their companies are those who have a certain flair for acting.

Perhaps one of the best illustrations of the self-discipline and acting ability required in the Outrageous Price Process is the movie classic *The Sting.* Paul Newman and Robert Redford master the art of the elaborate bluff by attending to every detail. Even simple hand gestures have critical meaning. While the Outrageous Price Process is certainly not illegal in any way, it does require the same sort of planning, an ability to keep cool under pressure, and an ability to adhere to a carefully created but constantly evolving strategy.

Like Newman and Redford, you and your advisers will play parts in a meticulously created plan that must be executed to perfection. You and your investment banker will play leading roles, but your attorney, your accountant, and perhaps key employees will also play cameo roles. Everyone in the "cast" must maintain a tone of casual nonchalance, or the plan will crumble. You and your advisers must consistently convey the "we don't care if we sell today, tomorrow, or ever" message.

Your investment banker must give a flawless performance (phone call after phone call, in each and every e-mail and text message, and at every meeting), while you play a more limited role. Every move in the negotiation is keyed off the buyer's reactions. Your strategy will be tweaked constantly, and at times you will need to play a part in a constantly evolving plan. Exactly what you say and how you say it show your buyer that your company is worth every penny of the price you are asking. You and your investment banker must unnerve the buyer with your conviction without ever being offensive or provoking the buyer's anger. Everyone on your team must be absolutely credible and "on message" at all times.

Before we look at specific attitudes you'll be asked to assume, let's deal with the credibility issue. If buyers suspect that you or your advisers are anything less than 100 percent legitimate, they will walk. You and your advisers must be true to your word. In order to do that, you and your advisers will choose precise words and tones to deliver information. Of course, you are expected to supply complete financial information to back up every claim you make. At every step of the process, your credibility and that of your advisers should grow in the buyer's eyes. You must be credible in each and every small thing, or you will not be believed in the big things. Remember that you are selling a multi-million-dollar vision of what the company could be worth to a buyer.

As critical as integrity is to any sale, it is especially critical during a sale for an Outrageous Price. As we've seen, the Outrageous Price Process involves demonstrating to a buyer the gain or pain that it could *potentially* experience if it purchases, or fails to purchase, your company. When we talk about potential, the buyer makes assumptions about what it might do if it acquires the seller or what the seller might do if the buyer walks away. There is no way sellers can be completely transparent about what they intend (or do not intend) to do—during the sale process. That's the line we draw: Credibility must be maintained at all times. Transparency, however, is an unrealistic ground rule for any business transaction. Based on his or her experience, your investment banker makes countless judgment calls during the course of a deal about exactly where that line is.

In explaining this difference between credibility and transparency to sellers, I often use the analogy of dating. On a first date, no one is expected to reveal every skeleton in one's closet. (Those who do never experience a second date, much less marriage!) As the dating process progresses and the parties become more comfortable with each other, each party begins to reveal some of the less glamorous aspects of their lives: the lazy ex-husband, crazy ex-wife, or substance-abuse habit kicked. As each party becomes more invested in the other, these blemishes are more easily put into context. Each party is free to decide whether a particular blemish (or the entire package) is one they can or cannot live with.

So it is in business sales. We are honest about the blemishes that may exist, but we reveal them only as the deal progresses. We are entirely credible without being entirely and immediately transparent.

Acting Attitude #1: Selling? Not Today, Thanks.

In the Outrageous Price Process, sellers assume the "no need to sell" attitude. In the typical competitive auction, the investment banker advertises a company for sale. In the Outrageous Price Process, however, the goal of "marketing" the company is simply to attract the buyer's attention. That must be done without advertising and without even mentioning a sale price. As you can imagine, this requires significant creativity on the part of your investment banker. (We discussed various strategies to attract the attention of an Outrageous Buyer in Chapter 8.)

Once you've attracted a buyer's attention (a buyer who is susceptible to significant pain or gain in purchasing your company), you make that buyer aware of how your company can alleviate that pain or capitalize on its gain without being obvious. We don't call the prospective buyer and sell the value of owning your company, as might happen in an ordinary sale. Instead, we might give the impression that you are interested in making an acquisition, when selling is your ultimate intent. The goal is to cause a deep-pocketed buyer to realize that unless it buys your company it faces a serious threat to its business or forgoes an opportunity for tremendous gain.

Remember the example of the steel post company? Saint Louis Post's repeated holiday sales sent the message "We can and will undercut your prices and upset the market." In the case of Wisconsin Medical Waste, securing additional permits in major metropolitan areas kept the target buyer wondering what WMW was up to and supported its suspicion that perhaps WMW intended to expand.

No matter what particular strategy you and your investment banker create to take you to the Outrageous Price, sellers must act as if they will execute that strategy. Once sellers attract a target buyer's attention, they must maintain complete credibility. In the example of the steel post company, we demonstrated to the buyer that Saint Louis Post could and would make a significant dent in the buyer's market. At a minimum, Saint Louis Post alienated the buyer's customers by significantly undercutting its price. At the buyer's request, we allowed it to visit the plant and we made subtle, but deliberate, references to Saint Louis Post's financial fitness.

The post plant was in impeccable condition (thanks to thorough preparation, of course). We showed off the company's competitive advantage, in this case the technology, which enabled Saint Louis Post to make steel posts at a greatly reduced cost. We made sure the buyer knew that this owner had the capital to expand. Our message was clear: "We have the ability to undercut your margins significantly and thrive."

Acting Attitude #2: Never Let Them See You Sweat

Do you know how you react under pressure? Can you maintain a believable poker face? Not everyone can. If controlling your voice is a problem, someone else can do the majority of talking during emotionally charged moments. If you tap your fingers when you are uneasy, learn to keep your hands off the table. If you smoke, know that buyers recognize lighting up as a dead giveaway for nervousness and insecurity.

Whether you are aiming for the Outrageous Price or just seeking to sell your company, trusting your adviser, exercising self-discipline, and becoming a credible actor are all key ingredients in the success of your sale. If you choose the best adviser, he or she will help prepare you for your role in the negotiations that lie ahead, but the adviser cannot go after the Outrageous Price alone. Having the right company to sell to the right buyer is only part of the equation: *You* have to have what it takes to sell for an Outrageous Price.

10

Pillar IV:
The Outrageous Adviser

So far, we've assembled the following ingredients, or pillars, for the Outrageous Price Process:

1. A successful company with a competitive advantage (the ability to do or make something better or more cheaply than all of its competitors) and a direct relationship between the seller's competitive advantage and a buyer's need that may be able to be leveraged to persuade the buyer to pay handsomely to acquire the company from the seller

2. A buyer with enough financial firepower to pay an Outrageous Price in order to purchase significant future gain or avoid significant pain

3. An owner who has the ability to trust his or her adviser, the guts and self-discipline to ride the roller coaster all the way to the end, and a certain flair for playing a role

We now add to our recipe another key ingredient, Pillar IV, a transaction adviser:

- With *experience* creating successful strategies to get Outrageous Prices for sellers
- With the *intelligence and analytical skills* to play the multilevel chess game that the Outrageous Price Process demands
- Who has the highly developed *people skills* to intuitively understand and predict behavior

Before we look at each of these characteristics more closely, a word to those owners who may be tempted to orchestrate the sale of their companies without assistance: *Don't do it!*

I am amazed at the number of business owners who attempt to sell their companies without outside assistance yet would never dream of designing a plant, an employee incentive plan, or a national marketing program without the assistance of skilled professionals. These same go-it-alone owners will use a real estate agent to sell their homes but will sell their companies to the competitor that has offered a "reasonable" market price. Other owners would stubbornly rather shut their doors than hire a professional to help them sell the most valuable asset they own.

Selling a company is a complex financial and legal transaction and therefore requires the services of accountants and attorneys. These professionals, however, are not generally trained in how to value a company for sale under current market conditions, set a sale price, find and evaluate buyers, or manage the complex negotiations required to get an owner the best possible price. For that, owners look to transaction intermediaries and must choose either a business broker or an investment banker.

The primary differences between a business broker and an investment banker are (1) business brokers do not work in the same value arena as investment bankers and (2) the two disciplines employ very different sale processes.

BUSINESS BROKERS

Business brokers typically represent companies worth less than $5 million. They generally hold real estate licenses and do not orchestrate either competitive auctions or Outrageous Price sales. These intermediaries broadcast "for sale" announcements far and wide and, like real estate agents, direct interested parties to any one of their listings.

If your company is in the $5 million value range and you think that it is a candidate for either a competitive auction or the Outrageous Price Process, you should interview investment bankers. Business brokers do not orchestrate these types of sales because companies worth less than $5 million do not attract the well-financed buyers that participate in competitive auctions and pay Outrageous Prices.

Well-financed buyers seek characteristics not generally found in smaller companies, such as proven and motivated management teams, strong financial controls, straightforward accounting, effective operating systems, stable and increasing cash flow, realistic growth strategies, and diversified customer bases. The buyers needed for a successful competitive auction or Outrageous Price Process are not willing to devote the time necessary to install any of these attributes in return for minimal impact on their bottom lines.

You can expect to find a number of business brokers in most metropolitan areas, but successful ones are few—too few, in fact, to serve the number of business owners who need their services. Please don't infer that successful brokers are rare for any other reason than that they face a daunting economic task. In return for a fee of approximately $5,000 to $150,000, the business broker is asked to work with often-unreliable financial records, attract a less-than-well-financed buyer, and cross swords with skilled buyer representatives. In short, brokers perform a more difficult job, for less money, than do investment bankers. This job description does not attract a large number of applicants.

INVESTMENT BANKERS

If your company exceeds the $5 million threshold and you are interested in selling via a competitive auction or the Outrageous Price Process, you'll want to retain an investment banker. Not all investment bankers, however, are skilled in all types of sales, so the question is: What kind of investment banker do you need to orchestrate the sale of your company either through a negotiated sale, a competitive auction, or the Outrageous Price Process?

Level One Investment Bankers

While most investment bankers are experienced in creating competitive auctions, not all are. Many investment bankers (those I call Level One investment bankers) mirror the activities of the business broker for a larger fee. Like business brokers, Level One investment bankers list companies for sale and attempt to attract as much attention as possible to all of their listings. Only in rare cases does this type of investment banker (or business broker) spend significant time creating sales or marketing strategies for one particular company. Once a potential buyer expresses interest in a listing, the broker or Level One banker works with that buyer to achieve the seller's asking price.

Level Two Investment Bankers

This is the category into which most investment bankers fall. They are more than highly paid business brokers, but they aren't experienced in creating sales resulting in Outrageous Prices.

Investment bankers in this category understand valuations, the financial formulas incorporated into spreadsheets, and the legal concepts important in transferring a company. They know how to sell a company based on the results listed on its balance sheet and profit and loss statements.

Like their Level One counterparts, Level Two investment bankers may not orchestrate many deals. In fact, most have not done more than five deals in the past five years. These bankers are often retired from larger investment banking firms or from positions in corporate finance.

To determine if the investment banker you interview conducts competitive auctions, you have to do some research, talk to former clients who have used that method, and ask questions. Look up the investment banker's company in Investment Dealers' Digest's or FactSet Mergerstat's annual listings of investment banking activity.

Call or meet with the investment banker's former clients. (See Appendix D, "Checking an Investment Banker's References," for a list of questions you can ask an investment banker's former clients.) Ask the investment banker how many competitive auctions he or she has conducted in the past twelve months. (The answer you are looking for is at least five.) Ask how much money he or she personally makes exclusively from M&A transaction fees. (Here the answer is at least $2 million per year.) Ask your professional advisers if this investment banker is well known and well respected in his or her community. Finally, look at the big picture: Does the investment banker's office reflect a multi-million-dollar practice?

Outrageous Price Investment Bankers

This is a good news/bad news situation for the owner looking for an investment banker skilled in Outrageous Price sales. The bad news is that there are very few investment bankers who know how to orchestrate this type of sale. The good news is that if you find one, you have hit the jackpot.

Why can so few investment bankers orchestrate the Outrageous Price Process? For some insight, let's look first at the basic methodology used by the Outrageous Price investment banker.

1. The Outrageous Price investment banker dives into the company to uncover its competitive advantage(s).
2. Having identified that company's unique competitive advantage(s), the investment banker creates, through exhaustive research, a list of buyers that would significantly benefit if they purchased the selling company (or would significantly suffer if they did not).
3. The Outrageous Price investment banker then carefully crafts a strategy designed to persuade the target buyer that it is well worth paying an Outrageous Price to acquire the company for sale.

Level Two investment bankers skip the tedious process of identifying the competitive advantage and, instead, rely on the traditional sale method: Instruct an analyst or intern to bundle the financials into a good-looking book, then send the book to potential buyers. The Level Two investment banker answers buyer questions, negotiates the deal, and collects a fee. Not only is this method the path of least resistance, it is a great way to make money because it requires minimal time on the part of the investment banker. Because not every company has one (much less two or three) competitive advantage(s), few investment bankers take the time to search for them, know how to find them, and enjoy both tasks. Only those investment bankers who enjoy the challenge of mining for the gold nugget pursue the Outrageous Price.

Of the handful of investment bankers who enjoy the challenge, only a rare few *know how to apply competitive advantage to a business sale.* Because Michael Porter's theory on competitive advantage is taught in most business schools, most investment bankers are able to recite its definition. If you want to find out whether your company is a candidate for an Outrageous Price, however, you must find the investment banker who not only *has the desire* to do the hard work of successfully uncovering one (much less several) competitive advantage(s), but also understands how to leverage competitive advantage to get an Outrageous Price.

Questions that lead to identification of the competitive advantage include:

- Why is your company able to make a product more cheaply than anyone else?
- Why does it have a lock on market share in a geographical area?
- Why do customers perceive your company's product/service to be more valuable than that of your competitors?
- Have you created barriers that your competitors can't or won't surmount?

After asking detailed questions designed exclusively for your company, Outrageous Price investment bankers draw upon their experience to test your answers against what they've seen work for companies like yours. Finally, they'll put your answers into the context of your business (its manufacturing, distribution, and marketing systems) to determine if your company really does enjoy a competitive advantage. (For a more detailed explanation of the process of uncovering a competitive advantage, please see Chapter 4.) The Outrageous Price investment banker is the rare bird who knows how to leverage the competitive advantage and match it to a buyer's need.

Unless your investment banker understands exactly why your company is successful, he or she can't know which buyer would benefit or explain to that buyer exactly how buying your company will bring it outrageous gain or relieve it from outrageous pain. In short, this investment banker doesn't have what it takes to get an Outrageous Price for your company.

PEOPLE SKILLS

People skills may well be the first among equals on a list of investment banker characteristics because they are so critical to a seller's success. As mentioned in Chapter 9, owners who successfully achieve Outrageous Prices for their companies must be able to trust—without reservation—their investment bankers. Your job as a seller is to find the adviser deserving of that trust. As you interview prospective advisers, you may not be able to gauge their raw intelligence or judgment, but you will quickly get a feel for an adviser's people skills.

Understanding People

Chemistry between you and your investment banker is important, but you are not looking for a new best buddy. Neither are you looking for the easiest-going, best backslapper you've ever met. When evaluating people skills, you are looking for someone who observes each player (you, your other advisers, the buyer, and the buyer's advisers) at the table so carefully that he or she can sense what each is thinking and feeling. That keen observation enables your investment banker to predict behavior, adapt his or her behavior to the situation at hand, and draw out information.

Predicting Behavior

A good investment banker has what many sellers judge to be an uncanny ability to predict behavior. In reality there's nothing mysterious about making accurate predictions. Not only do good investment bankers have loads of experience in deal making and a personal (and often lifelong) interest in the study of human nature and personality types; they know how to predict what others will do by examining their past moves. Not surprisingly, investment bankers who listen more than they talk are often the best at predicting behavior.

As you travel the road to an Outrageous Price or participate in a competitive auction, there are numerous opportunities for bluffing—on both sides. Buyers almost always threaten to walk from the deal unless A, B, or C happens. (Inevitably, A, B, or C equals a significant drop in price!) The investment banker must be able to react appropriately to each bluff so that sellers get the outcomes they want. For example, some buyers always respond negatively the first time a proposal is made. Making the proposal to these same buyers a second or third time elicits a positive response. In other cases, buyers prefer to split the difference. If we offer a $500,000 concession on an issue and the buyer wants $1 million, a split-the-difference buyer usually accepts $750,000.

Adapting to Behavior

Your investment banker not only should be able to predict buyers' reactions, but must also be able to adapt to each. There is no playbook for handling transactions, buyers, communication, or negotiating points. Using a strategy successfully once does not guarantee its future success because there are too many moving parts in a transaction to draw a direct cause-and-effect relationship. For that reason, your investment banker must have not only significant experience, but also the ability to adapt to a constantly changing environment.

Your investment banker must be able to respond to a wide range of temperaments as well. For example, negotiating with a CEO is quite different from negotiating with a CFO. Each values different benefits of the deal, and your investment banker needs to know what they are and how best to sell these benefits. Chief executive officers generally focus on the competitive advantages or on *synergies.* Usually, these synergies include acquiring a greater percentage of the market or protecting existing market share, eliminating a competitor, or acquiring a complementary line of distribution. On the other hand, chief financial officers focus on the financial ramifications of the deal and the financial justifications for the asking price.

Further, buyers use different negotiating styles. One might use intimidation to score points, while another uses an incremental "inching" approach. Whether the heat in the kitchen rises quickly or slowly, if your investment banker can't handle the heat, get out. Fast.

Drawing Out Information

Controlling the flow of information in a competitive auction or in the quest for the Outrageous Price is a key element of the multilevel chess game your investment banker plays with a buyer. (We'll look at what's involved in that chess game in a moment.) Most transaction advisers know how to disseminate information, but you want to hire the investment banker who is skilled in drawing information out of others. You want the banker who orchestrates each interaction so he or she leaves the table with more information than the other party.

To gauge this ability, after you interview prospective bankers ask yourself who learned more about whom? Did the investment banker talk about him- or herself or elicit information from you about your goals, your company, and possibly your preferences and fears? Do you think that the investment banker left the table knowing what makes you tick and why you scheduled the meeting? That's the kind of insight you want the investment banker to have into the people he or she will be negotiating with on your behalf. Your investment banker must understand who is at the negotiating table and why.

One of the ways an investment banker gathers information is to purposely omit it. For example, an average deal book provides prospective buyers as much positive information as possible to attract their attention. A better deal book prompts interested buyers to ask more specific questions. For example, it may include information about the number of a company's U.S. customers but provide no detail about exactly where those customers are located. When a prospective buyer calls the investment banker to ask exactly how many customers are in the western region, the investment banker learns something interesting about what is important to that buyer.

Strategic Salesmanship

There are thousands of books written about sales philosophies, sales strategies, and sales techniques. As a successful business owner, you've probably read quite a few, but, more important, you know the techniques that work best for you. In the context of evaluating the sales expertise of an investment banker, however, what works best for you may or may not be the same skills your investment banker will use in a sales transaction. Fundamentally, you are looking for the investment banker who can listen well and who can speak persuasively. Let's look at a few basics of sales techniques for investment bankers.

Attribute 1: Tells Great Stories

There are a number of speaking abilities that contribute to salesmanship, but the one most important to an investment banker is the ability to tell a compelling story. In the case of getting an Outrageous Price for an ordinary company, you are asking an investment banker to persuade a buyer—who has likely never heard of your company—to buy your company (warts and all) for an Outrageous Price because the buyer is convinced (as a result of your investment banker's efforts) that doing so is the best decision it will ever make. If that's not a definition of moving mountains, what is?

Mountain-moving investment bankers have excellent oral and written communication skills. They can compose e-mail messages or advertisements—without sacrificing your confidentiality—that compel prospective buyers to respond. They know how to frame difficult topics in a way that elicits the most favorable response. Given that there are no do-overs in the sale process, these investment bankers get it right first time, every time.

To find the investment banker who can move mountains, listen carefully to how the investment banker communicates with you during your initial meetings. Ask for samples of e-mail messages and a deal book from a completed sale. Put yourself in a prospective buyer's shoes: Would the story in the e-mail messages or the deal book catch and hold your attention?

Attribute 2: Designs Creative Marketing Strategies

In addition to speaking and writing persuasively, you are looking for an investment banker whose plan to market your company goes beyond the traditional three-step method:

1. Pull twenty or so top prospects from a purchased database.
2. Send prospects a book describing the company for sale.
3. Wait for offers.

Pass by these "order takers" to find an investment banker who has invested in the back-office support—a research staff—that constantly updates its database of private equity groups and strategic buyers. There is nothing wrong with purchased lists if they are simply the starting point for constant updating and research.

From those lists, the investment banker can create a unique list of possible buyers for your company and convey basic information (using no names or identifiable information) in a variety of ways. E-mail communications, advertisements for trade journals, and hard-copy mailings can all be carefully designed to attract the interest of qualified buyers.

The adviser you choose should be interested enough in the marketing aspect of his or her job to be constantly evaluating the success of various marketing techniques. Getting the word out to as many potential buyers as possible may make your transaction adviser's job more costly and complex, but it exponentially increases your chances of closing for an Outrageous Price.

Attribute 3: Is Sensitive to Confidentiality

Few investment bankers are as concerned about your confidentiality as you are. It is not in their interest to be. They get paid to close deals. If in doing so they disclose more about your company than you might prefer, they lose nothing.

That said, how do you find an investment banker who puts your confidentiality at the top of his or her priority list? First, ask references if there were any breaches in confidentiality and ask if they originated with the investment banker or the banker's firm.

Second, ask the investment banker for a confidentiality plan. Expect a detailed explanation (usually verbal) of the processes—both external and internal—he or she uses to maintain confidentiality. The plan should include in-house procedures that cover invoices (what they say and where they are sent), telephone contact (the number used to contact the seller and exactly how messages are conveyed), and how the investment banking firm identifies itself to the seller's employees. The plan should cover external procedures that govern how the investment banker's firm communicates with your other advisers and prospective buyers.

While the investment banker may not put those procedures in writing, you should expect a written evaluation that classifies buyers in terms of threat: If a prospective buyer learns confidential information about your company, would that buyer pose no threat, some potential threat, or a definite threat? In the "definite threat" category are competitors who, if given a hint of a sale, would declare open season on your customers and employees. "Potentially dangerous" buyers are more sensitive prospects who can't be completely trusted so are given information only on a limited basis and with very little time to respond. They are brought into the game only if the buyers in the first group aren't offering as much money as would buyers in this second group.

Once classified according to threat potential, you and your investment banker then determine how much information to provide buyers in each classification and how much time to give those buyers to respond. For example, a buyer who poses a potential threat may be given only very limited information (an abbreviated deal book) with little time to respond.

Finally, the level of threat a class of buyer poses directly affects when, during the course of a deal, that buyer is contacted. For example, if a selling company has significant confidentiality issues (either the owner is hypersensitive or information could identify the company), during the first phase of the marketing process the investment banker contacts only those buyers that pose no threat. Usually, this nonthreatening group includes private equity groups that aren't in the selling company's industry and have no vested interest in leaking word of a sale to the seller's competitors.

During the second marketing phase, the investment banker contacts those buyers that pose a potential threat. Again, the investment banker tailors information to this more threatening group of buyers. He or she may remove customer data or intellectual property information. The investment banker can mask gross profit data or omit entirely cost advantage information that could do great damage in the hands of your customers.

Only when buyers in these first groups are actively negotiating offers should your investment banker even consider contacting those buyers that pose a definite threat to your company. If you and your investment banker decide to contact buyers in this last group, you will do so only because it is likely that one of them will pay more than any other buyer, or that buyer's presence in the process will motivate other buyers to pay more.

You want to work with an investment banker who understands your confidentiality concerns well enough to create a strategy that makes you comfortable. The following chart is an example of a threat/confidentiality matrix.

Threat/Confidentiality Matrix

Type of Buyer	Information Provided	Timing of Contact
Nonthreatening	Carefully stated with enough detail to spark interest	Immediately
Potential threat	Provide very limited information requiring very short response time	After nonthreatening buyers respond with expressions of interest
Definite threat	None	Extremely rarely

For each tier, expect the investment banker to create a corresponding and appropriate strategy to reach these buyers and to design specific techniques to convey and protect information. For example, the banker may create several deal books, one tailored to each tier, or no deal book at all.

If an investment banker responds to your questions about confidentiality by assuring you that he or she requires prospective buyers to sign nondisclosure agreements, probe further. What you want to know is whether the investment banker enforces them. For example, if your investment banker hears that a prospective buyer has shared information with a competitor or even a noninterested party, does the banker call that buyer? Does the banker call you to let you know what has occurred?

Attribute 4: Listens Attentively

Earlier in this chapter, we talked about the investment banker's ability to elicit information from the party across the table. We return to that issue here because it is an important sales strategy of the Outrageous Price investment banker.

In the sale of a company for an Outrageous Price, the sale is not ultimately about the facts. Of course, the Outrageous Price sale starts with its feet squarely based in fact (value, sales numbers, profits, market share, EBITDA, etc.), but it quickly goes airborne in a leap of faith.

Let's say that the prevailing multiple for a company like yours in today's market is three times EBITDA, and all the facts (valuation, etc.) support that price. You and your investment banker decide, however, that because your company has a unique competitive advantage of great value to Company X, you believe the value to this buyer is nine times EBITDA.

While it is critical that your investment banker say the right things to persuade Company X to pay a higher price, he or she must also possess the ability to listen to Company's X's objections and fears. Only by listening can your investment banker overcome Company X's objections or fears. Only by listening can your investment banker understand if the Company X executive spearheading this deal is afraid of losing his or her job if the deal fails to goes through. Only by listening can your investment banker address Company X's worst-case and what-if scenarios. As you interview prospective investment bankers, take time to evaluate their listening skills.

INTELLIGENCE AND ANALYTICAL SKILLS

Selling a company using a competitive auction or for an Outrageous Price is much like playing a multilevel game of chess. Before making a move, we analyze how that move will affect every other player in the transaction, the entire subsequent sequence of moves, and the end result. We also consider every possible response that a buyer could make and estimate the probability of each. We then determine exactly how we will react to each response because it is important to be able to say to a buyer, "I've already thought about that and . . ." If an investment banker is prepared for every possible buyer move, sellers enjoy a much stronger negotiating position.

Finally, as in chess, your investment banker should focus on behavior— what buyers actually do—rather than on their words. Inexperienced bankers are often distracted by all the talking buyers do, forgetting that the truth is in the action.

You need an experienced investment banker who has the intelligence and analytical skills to survive and succeed at this game. A successful deal maker has (1) the ability to anticipate how each move affects future moves, (2) the ability to understand and skillfully manage numbers, and (3) the ability to evaluate deal structures in light of your goals.

Anticipating Future Challenges

The ability to anticipate future challenges is one aspect of winning the game of chess. Good players know that most opponents attempt well-known, and often successful, strategies. In the transaction world, investment bankers anticipate that buyers will do the same. Specifically, they will try to lower the purchase price in a process we call *retrading*. (Please see Chapter 3 for more information about common retrading issues.)

In a competitive auction with multiple buyers bidding simultaneously (described in Chapter 11), your investment banker can simply eliminate from the auction the buyer who tries to lower its offer. Elimination is a hugely effective arrow in your investment banker's quiver. In the Outrageous Price Process, however, there is often just one buyer. In that case, not only is that buyer highly motivated to manufacture items to "justify" a lower purchase price; your investment banker doesn't have the luxury of eliminating that buyer from the process. The only ace in your investment banker's hand is your willingness to walk away from the deal if it does not meet your terms. It is critically important, then, that your investment banker have the experience and insight necessary to anticipate, prepare for, and overcome the buyer's demands without playing that card unless it is absolutely necessary.

Understanding and Managing Numbers

Preparing company tax returns and profit and loss statements, proposing tax-saving strategies, and defending you during an audit are not the financial skills you need from your investment banker. Instead, the adviser who orchestrates the sale of your company must be able to discover, comprehend, and tell the story (using numbers) of how your company's competitive advantage will benefit it.

The investment banker must uncover your company's competitive advantage, and do it in a fairly short period of time. Second, the investment banker must figure out how your company's competitive advantage benefits (or hurts) the buyer with the deepest pockets. Finally, he or she must clearly and persuasively communicate the potential gain or pain to that potential buyer.

To gauge an investment banker's proficiency at understanding and managing numbers, take a step back and observe how well the investment banker explains complex topics. If you find these explanations to be too obtuse or too wordy, know that the investment banker's explanations to potential buyers will be the same. You want an investment banker who understands your company completely, who has great sales skills, and who can articulate complex issues in a way which others easily understand.

If you are interested in pursuing the Outrageous Price, you require not only an investment banker who is a quick study and who can persuade you to hire him or her, but also one who offers new insights into your company. Look for the investment banker who, within the first thirty minutes of your initial meeting, says something about your business model or a pressing business issue that took you ten years to figure out. Hire the one who shows you that he or she understands not *how* your business works but *why* your business works.

Meeting Your Goals

At the end of the day, you want to hire the investment banker who does not attempt to close the deal with the first buyer but who negotiates the best possible terms from each buyer in light of *your* goals. Further, when there is more than one offer, sellers likely require some help comparing and quantifying the differences among them. In a competitive auction, one buyer may offer more gross dollars and agree to keep your son in his current position but require you to carry a promissory note. Another offers fewer dollars but allows you to retain your health and retirement benefits at no cost. Still another offers more money than either, but will only purchase your company's assets rather than its stock.

As the number of combinations increases, your banker should prioritize offers in light of your goals and create strategies for each buyer designed to improve their offers. There are many investment bankers who simply collect offers and let the seller pick the best one. Look for advisers with the work ethic and creativity necessary to get the best price, the smarts and desire to prioritize issues according to your goals, and the willingness to work in your interest rather than in their own.

EXPERIENCE

I purposely left experience to the end of this chapter because most owners readily understand what an important quality it is. They know what a difference it makes in their own lives. Experience is also easier to quantify than are people skills, sales expertise, or intelligence and analytical skills. Most investment bankers list transactions on their websites; you can talk to their references, learn the number of years they've been in the business, and check national rankings (such as Thomson Reuters FactSet Mergerstat, and Investment Dealers' Digest).

Beyond quantity, however, there is the issue of quality. If you are to pursue the Outrageous Price for your company, have the years of experience equipped this investment banker to take you there? Let's look at several lessons that only experience can teach.

The Competitive Advantage

In Chapter 4 and Chapter 7, we talked about how absolutely necessary it is that your investment banker find and leverage your company's competitive advantage in order to achieve an Outrageous Price for your company. Rather than repeat that discussion here, note only that if an investment banker does not know how to uncover and use a company's competitive advantage to structure a transaction, keep looking.

Reputation

You know that the reputation of a transaction adviser is a direct result of his or her experience. What you may not appreciate is how directly that reputation impacts your chances of getting the best possible price for your company. Let's look briefly at the two arenas where your investment banker operates: the professional community and the buyer marketplace.

Professional community. To sell your company using either the competitive auction or the Outrageous Price Process you must choose an investment banker whose reputation allows him or her to attract the top-tier talent (from the legal and accounting world) that you need to complete the sale successfully.

Especially in the Outrageous Price Process, not only must all participating advisers be responsive to tight deadlines and experienced in third-party transactions, but they should also be experts in their professions. If your investment banker does not have an excellent reputation in the professional community, he or she won't be able to attract this type of adviser.

Whether you plan to sell using a competitive auction or for an Outrageous Price, expect the buyer to try to discredit the investment banker and other members of your transaction team. Doing so is just another ploy that buyers use to chisel away at the purchase price and undermine your confidence in your asking price. When you hire a reputable investment banker and the best possible advisers, you can neutralize these attempts.

If you do pursue an Outrageous Price for your company, you can be absolutely sure that the buyer will call its contacts in your banker's community to ask, quite bluntly, if your investment banker is crazy. ("Does this nut job really think he can get $20 million for a company worth $10 million on a good day?") Buyers make such calls to partners in major law firms to find out if they have ever heard of the banker, and if so, what they have heard. You want those pillars of the legal community to have heard of your investment banker for all the right reasons.

Buyer marketplace. In addition to a sterling reputation in the professional community, your investment banking firm should have a solid reputation among buyers. In a competitive auction, the investment banker must have credibility in the eyes of private equity groups or they will steer clear of your deal. If they don't completely ignore your investment banker (the most likely scenario) and do enter into negotiations, they will likely assume that your banker doesn't know what he or she is doing. Further, the PEG will believe little that an unknown investment banker says. For example, if an unknown investment banker proposes a creative solution to a sticky problem, the PEG will likely ignore the input.

In the Outrageous Price Process, it is unlikely that the Outrageous Buyer will know your investment banker, but rest assured that it will investigate his or her background. Outrageous Buyers are professionals, and they do their homework. Expect them to contact partners of major law and accounting firms in the area in which the investment banker does business.

If your investment banker enjoys less than a good reputation in the marketplace, it is not unusual for the president of a corporate division or the lead adviser for a PEG to assume that the owner who hires that banker is of dubious character as well. If a prospective buyer decides to pursue the sale regardless of these concerns, you can be sure that it will check, double-check, and triple-check every piece of information from the seller. The buyer will not grant any benefit of the doubt to the seller.

Most important to you, however, is that an investment banker with no reputation or a poor reputation will not have the credibility needed when he or she tells the prospective buyer that there are other buyers at the table. You need that vital leverage to get the best possible offer from every buyer. If your investment banker has no credibility, you simply cannot pursue the Outrageous Price or benefit from this greatest attribute of the competitive auction process.

Check an investment banker's reputation with your accountant, attorney, or banker before you spend time interviewing. If you are thinking of hiring an investment banker outside of your community, ask your advisers to check with their colleagues in the investment banker's community.

Unfortunately, there is no accrediting organization for transaction intermediaries, nor is there an established set of ethical standards.

Understanding Buyers

There is no substitute for experience when it comes to understanding buyers. While it is not necessary for your investment banker to have represented buyers in order to understand them, it does help. What's more important is that your investment banker ask you the probing, insightful, and creative questions that reveal the types of buyers who would profit from owning your company. Expect questions about your customers, suppliers, and competitors. But also look for the investment banker to offer new ideas about businesses that share your company's customer base. If the investment banker simply restates what you've said, you should move on to the next interview.

Another facet of understanding buyers is to have had enough experience with them to understand their limits. For example, a common mistake of rookie negotiators is to fail to recognize when they are in hot water. Water temperature increases quickly when investment bankers underestimate the skill of their opponents, when they fail to prepare meticulously, or, most often, when ego prevents them from asking the right questions.

Ability to Discriminate

The ability to discriminate between serious and nonserious buyers is another function of your investment banker's experience and judgment. Let's say that your investment banker takes your company to market and receives twenty-six expressions of interest. The investment banker must then analyze each offer to uncover the one serious buyer who will offer you the best terms. Unless your investment banker is a mind reader, he or she draws upon experience to develop a series of tests designed to sift the wheat from the chaff. Tests that I find highly predictive are ones that require buyers to spend money. For example, which buyers are willing to make trips to your location? Which hire accountants to perform due diligence?

There are a million ways to back out of a deal, so finding the one buyer who is excited about the deal and will stay until the end is the real art.

Maintaining Deal Momentum

As Chapter 11 discusses (in the section headed "The Competitive Auction"), a lack of speed is one of a buyer's best allies. The more time a buyer has to sift through and analyze a seller's information, the more time it has to dissimilate, attempt to reduce the purchase price, and assemble its land mines designed to detonate later in the sale process.

Experienced investment bankers know that buyers, like all predators, are apt to move more quickly and purposefully if there are competitors in the vicinity. Multiple buyers give sellers leverage.

If you are pursuing the Outrageous Price, however, there won't be multiple Outrageous Buyers. There may be several other buyers with whom we negotiate separately. While playing chess on two levels, your investment banker must keep the deal moving. Experienced investment bankers first maintain their cool and conduct the process as if there is more than one buyer involved. Further, they are skilled in providing the sole buyer with deadlines—not ultimatums—using careful, professional wording, and they maintain constant contact.

Finally, experienced investment bankers never underestimate the skill of a buyer, understanding that, for the most part, buyers are professionals that make it their business to know the seller's financials better than the seller. Most owners don't believe this is so until they learn of the ticking time bomb that a buyer has inserted into either the letter of intent or the purchase agreement. This bomb is usually a formula designed to explode after the deal closes and cause maximum damage to the seller.

Experience, analytical skills, salesmanship, and people skills: These are qualities common to almost all successful investment bankers. If you are seeking an Outrageous Price for your company, however, you've got to find the investment banker who specializes in the Outrageous Price Process. Outrageous Price investment bankers have created Outrageous Price strategies for other companies and have *actually secured* Outrageous Prices for them. Their analytical skills are so sharp that they can identify why your company achieves the results it does (its competitive advantage) and can quickly leverage that competitive advantage into an Outrageous Price. Finally, investment bankers who sell companies for Outrageous Prices have people skills that go far beyond an easygoing and friendly nature. Outrageous Price investment bankers study, understand, and predict behavior. They can bond and adapt to a wide variety of personalities and know how to listen and frame questions designed to elicit more information than they give away.

These are the exceptional qualities your investment banker must have if you are to pursue the Outrageous Price.

WHAT TO EXPECT AT YOUR FIRST MEETING WITH AN INVESTMENT BANKER

Most owners arrive in my office as a result of a referral by their attorneys, CPAs, financial planners, insurance professionals, or another business owner. Prior to our first meeting, I will send the owner a signed nondisclosure agreement requiring that I keep confidential anything and everything we will

	Level One I-banker	Level Two I-banker	Outrageous Price I-banker
Deal size	$1 million to $10 million	$10 million to $250 million	$10 million to $250 million
Negotiated sales	X	X	X
Competitive auctions		X	X
Outrageous Price sales			X
Understanding People:		More likely	Most likely
• Predicting behavior			
• Adapting to behavior			
• Drawing out information			
Experience:			
• Using the competitive advantage			X
• Reputation		X	X
• Maintaining deal momentum		X	X

discuss at our first meeting. The agreement my firm uses requires us to maintain that owner's confidentiality whether or not the owner retains the firm. Typically, owners have their attorneys review the agreement before signing and returning it. (See Appendix F for a sample nondisclosure agreement between an owner and an investment banker.)

Some owners attend our first meeting alone, others bring the referring adviser, and still others bring a family member (usually a spouse). The purpose of this first meeting is for each of us to gauge our comfort level with the other.

I typically ask owners why they started their companies, about the history of their companies, their reasons for selling, their sale price expectations, and about their postsale life plans. Owners ask me about my company (how many deals we have negotiated over the past six or twelve months) and my experience in doing deal work (how many deals in which I have acted as lead negotiator). They often ask about my experience in dealing with companies like theirs, by which they mean similar in size or industry or ownership (family owned or entrepreneur led).

Many owners want to talk about their companies' financials, and often they want to talk about what makes their companies unique. Because identifying and leveraging a company's competitive advantage is so critical to the success of the transaction process I use, we often spend the bulk of our meeting talking about a company's unique characteristics.

In addition to the typical questions, I recommend that owners ask investment bankers the following questions:

1. Can you provide several references from the legal and accounting communities?
2. Can you provide names of owners whose companies you have sold?
3. Can you provide names of owners whose companies did not sell?
4. How many lawsuits have you and/or your company been engaged in with buyers or sellers?
5. Does your firm maintain its own research department and does it include research professionals, IT professionals, and financial analysts? If so, how many?
6. Is your firm nationally ranked on independent League Tables?

Let's look at each question more carefully.

Professional References

Most investment bankers are able to provide professional references; your job is to assess the quality of those references and ask those references the right questions. For example, does the investment banker communicate in a timely manner? Are all of the firm's communications (materials, conversations, etc.) professional? Did your client receive the attention you felt he or she deserved?

Client References

If an investment banker cannot provide names of past clients, there's a problem. The investment banker either has no experience as a lead negotiator or has no satisfied clients. If you receive names, you should create a list of questions for these former owners. You may want to know if the investment banker kept the owner in the loop, maintained strict confidentiality, and was nimble and creative during negotiations all while keeping the owner's goals at the top of the priority list.

Failed Deals

All investment bankers active in the M&A market have deals that did not close in their past. Your job is to find out why those deals did not close. Remember, there are perfectly legitimate reasons for failing to close, such as a significant decline in the seller's earnings.

Lawsuits

Your investment banker should be candid about how many lawsuits he or she has been involved in with past sellers or buyers. If the investment banker has been party to one or more suits, you want to know about the circumstances and about the results. If you suspect that your investment banker is being less than candid, keep looking for one you trust or insert in the engagement letter the representation that the investment banker and his or her firm have been party to no such suits.

Research

Many smaller and midsize firms do not maintain their own research or information technology departments. Because they have not made the investment in these areas, you will pay—either in the form of higher fees or in a lower-quality pool of buyers. Firms without these departments buy such services from outside contractors and pass the charges on to you. These services are often not as tailored to your needs as are those created by in-house departments.

League Tables

Independent organizations rank investment banks based on the dollar value of the transactions they have closed. Thomson Reuters, FactSet Mergerstat, and Investment Dealers Digest are three of the organizations that rank midsize investment banking firms. Check these rankings to see if the investment bank you are considering has the deal volume it claims.

Financial Reports

If an owner brings financial reports to our first meeting, I review those before our second meeting so I can present a thumbnail valuation of the company. At that meeting, we also talk about a sale price and about my fees. These items present both the owner and me with two great opportunities to take each other's measure. I suggest that you talk candidly with investment bankers you interview about the range of sale price they think they can attract, as well as their fee terms. The way they answer your questions (dogmatically or with flexibility) and negotiate with you gives you great insight into how they will negotiate with prospective buyers.

Engagement Letter

After that second meeting, we send an engagement letter to the business owner fully expecting it to be the subject of further negotiation. Rather than interrupt the flow of this chapter, please see Appendix E for items to consider in an engagement letter. Appendix E contains a fairly detailed description, so if you are considering entering into an engagement with an investment banker, spend a moment or two familiarizing yourself with the agreement that will govern the most important transaction of your life.

11

Executing the Sale

W e've arrived at the moment of truth. All the pieces from the Proactive Sale Strategy are in place.

1. Having completed your Sale Readiness Assessment, you have analyzed your exit options, imagined your ideal sale, worked out any family considerations, talked to your advisers, and brought the important constituency groups on board with your plan.
2. You have completed your presale due diligence by buffing and polishing every surface of your business. You've removed the cobwebs from every nook and cranny, you've done more than a little deep cleaning, and you can stand back and say, "I'd buy this business."
3. You understand (maybe for the first time) why your customers buy from you. You understand how your company differs from its competitors, and you've done everything possible to deepen the moats around your business.

4. You and your investment banker have cast a large net to find the most likely buyers for your company. You've rejected the buyers you will not consider and are open to the possibility that a buyer you had not identified may appear.

THE COMPETITIVE AUCTION

Let's assume that you are one of the lucky ones, and the Four Pillars of the Outrageous Price are in place as well.

- ◆ **Pillar I:** You and your investment banker have discovered a way to leverage your company's competitive advantage to either offer a prospective buyer tremendous gain or cause it pain it cannot ignore.
- ◆ **Pillar II:** There is an Outrageous Buyer active in the marketplace who you have reason to believe may be attracted to this transaction.
- ◆ **Pillar III:** You have the self-discipline and vision that it takes to pursue the Outrageous Price.
- ◆ **Pillar IV:** You've found an investment banker whom you trust and who understands how to orchestrate the Outrageous Price Process.

If all these pieces are in place, the best path is clear: Use a competitive auction to go for the Outrageous Price. In Chapter 7, we saw how three owners did exactly that to achieve a far-beyond-what-they-ever-expected result.

If, however, you are one of the majority of owners who complete the Proactive Sale Strategy only to find that one of the Four Pillars of the Outrageous Price is missing in action, what are your options?

A MISSING PILLAR

First, sit down with your investment banker for a candid discussion about the missing Outrageous Price pillar. If you postpone the sale by six months, twelve months, or two years, will that pillar still be MIA? And if not, can you wait that long to sell?

A Distracted Buyer

Let's assume that you have completed the Proactive Sale Process and, as you analyze whether you can pursue the Outrageous Price, you learn that the most logical Outrageous Buyer for your company is tied up in an ugly and very public lawsuit. You and your investment banker (one who has helped owners make these decisions before) have to ask whether the absence of this pillar can be mitigated.

◆ Can you wait for that buyer's attention to return to acquisitions?
◆ Can you return to your company focused on making it even more valuable (or even more annoying) to that particular buyer?
◆ Litigation can drag on. For how long are you willing to remain at the helm before you burn out?
◆ Is the industry you are in likely to stay vibrant over time?
◆ Are there economic factors beyond your control that could negatively affect your prospects for a sale? (Factors might include looming banking issues or worldwide economic turmoil.)

If prospects for the economy and your industry look favorable, and you can keep your company profitable for the number of months you expect it to take for this buyer to refocus, revisit your decision to sell in six months. If not, you can decide to go to market immediately and pursue the best possible price.

A Seller with a Pressing Need

After careful self-examination, you may realize that you could never take the necessary I-don't-need-to-sell attitude that sellers engaged in the Outrageous Price Process must be able to assume. You may be too tired, or you may have pressing health issues, or one of a million other reasons to want out too badly to convincingly pretend that you do not. Waiting six months, twelve months, or twelve years isn't going to change that. In this case, the absence of one pillar cannot be mitigated. What now?

If you and your investment banker decide that the time is right to go to market—even without the prospect of an Outrageous Price—by engaging in the Proactive Sale Strategy, you have already laid the best possible foundation for a successful sale. I strongly recommend that you capitalize on that foundation by using the sale process that gives you, as a seller, the most leverage and yields the best price the market will bear: the competitive auction.

No Leverageable Competitive Advantage

Not every company has a leverageable competitive advantage. Fewer still have advantages that we can leverage to extract an Outrageous Price from a buyer.

No Outrageous Price Investment Banker

This is a barrier many sellers encounter in their quests for the Outrageous Price. There may be other investment bankers who have observed, designed, and executed processes that lead to Outrageous Prices.

If you are one of those investment bankers, I'd love to hear from you. If, however, you are an owner who wants to take your best shot at an Outrageous Price, put your company through the Proactive Sale Strategy. Not only is it the platform from which we launch the Outrageous Price Process, it maximizes your chances of closing a deal at the best possible price.

COMPETITIVE AUCTION OR NEGOTIATED SALE?

In a competitive auction, multiple qualified buyers bid simultaneously to purchase a company. Negotiations occur across the table (between buyer and seller) and on the same side of the table (buyers compete with each other).

In a negotiated sale, one buyer faces off against one seller. Negotiations are conducted only across the table.

I meet many owners who already have, in hand, an "acceptable" offer from a buyer. They come not to launch a competitive auction but to see if I can improve the offer they have. Typically, these sellers are so concerned about their confidentiality that they prefer to negotiate with this one buyer and don't even want to talk about the advantages of marketing their companies to numerous prospective buyers.

Generally, this seller likes and trusts the prospective buyer and assumes that the process of selling the business will be similar to negotiating the sale of a home: (1) Buyer makes offer, (2) seller accepts offer, and (3) deal closes.

If you share this belief even after reading this book, I urge you to talk to former owners who have been through the sale process. Talk to any investment banker or transaction attorney, and, if they are honest, they will tell you that the smoothest transactions run off the rails at least five times. In typical transactions, the number is closer to ten. In addition to the numerous deal cripplers and deal killers that we described in Chapter 3, there are many other reasons for deals to falter or fail. Some of these obstacles include:

Seller's industry. If there is a significant change in the financial prospects of the seller's industry, buyers can and do scuttle deals.

Company profitability. Attaining a level of profitability comparable to (or exceeding) those of one's peers in the industry and maintaining profitability during the sale process seem to be intuitively obvious notions, and they are. But you would be amazed by how many owners take their eyes off profitability and focus instead on the sale process.

Quality of the management team. Buyers pay handsomely for successful, tested management teams. If you have any doubt about the quality, motivation, flexibility, or future performance of any member of your management team, I strongly recommend that, before taking the company to market, you retain an industrial psychology firm to assess these team members. The amount you spend retaining that firm is well worth keeping a deep-pocketed buyer at the table.

Gross margins. Like profitability, sellers must maintain their gross margins during the sale process. To do this, sellers must understand which customers "make" them the most money and resist the temptation, prior to the sale process, to increase sales by decreasing margins. Buyers look for this strategy and, when they discover it, at minimum, adjust the terms of the deal.

Customer concentration. Buyers are justifiably leery of purchasing companies in which only a few customers dominate the landscape. If no single customer accounts for more than 10 percent of gross sales, buyers are generally comfortable. At around 10 percent, red flags go up in a buyer's mind. When that percentage climbs to 20 to 30 percent, the deal can start to wobble, and at over 30 percent the company becomes unsaleable, the multiple changes (not in the seller's favor), or much of the cash at closing turns into various forms of earnouts.

Asset intensity. If your business requires a large amount of capital or equipment to generate its EBITDA, remember that a buyer will have to deploy an equally sizeable amount of capital to purchase that equipment to generate that same return. For example, a car dealership may have $10 million in inventory to generate $1 million in profit. If a buyer bases its purchase price on a multiple-of-earnings formula, it offsets the cost of acquiring a capital-intensive company in the purchase price.

Leverage of key employees. All of your critical employees, be they in management, sales, or research and development, have the potential to jeopardize a transaction if even one decides to hold you hostage or abandon ship before the deal closes. For that reason, I strongly recommend that owners ask these employees to sign stay bonus plans. (See that discussion in Chapter 2.)

Real estate. A real estate issue can run a deal off the rails if the owner has not accounted for its true cost. For example, if the company owns the real estate, the seller must normalize the EBITDA calculation by deducting a market rent for the facilities to accurately reflect the cost of occupancy. Similarly, if the real estate is owned outside of the company, EBITDA must also be adjusted (before taking the company to market) to accurately reflect the market rate.

In addition to hoping that the negotiated sale is as simple as 1, 2, 3, owners also assume that negotiating with one buyer will be:

◆ Far more confidential than any process involving multiple buyers
◆ Certainly faster than juggling multiple offers
◆ Much cheaper than negotiating with multiple buyers
◆ Less risky than negotiating with multiple buyers

Let's tackle these assumptions one at a time.

1. **Negotiating with one buyer is more confidential than negotiating with multiple buyers.** On an emotional level, sellers wish buyers would buy without ever seeing their companies. Intellectually, sellers know no buyer makes a "sight unseen" acquisition, but the war between the two positions rages in most sellers' heads.

Concern about confidentiality is a healthy thing. Information (or rumors) that prematurely leaks into the marketplace can be toxic to a seller's relationships with vendors, customers, and employees. But choosing the best sale process based on confidentiality concerns is myopic.

Of course, as the number of people who know of a sale increases so too can the risk of a breach of confidentiality. That's why we employ every possible technique to prevent leaks. But consider for a moment that it takes only *one person* to spill the beans about a sale, and the bean spiller may just as easily be the sole buyer as one of several.

Use your concerns about confidentiality to motivate you in your search for the investment banker who understands, takes seriously, and acts on your concerns.

- Does the investment banker extensively negotiate each nondisclosure agreement and tailor each NDA to each prospective buyer?
- Does the firm maintain a virtual data room, where access to your company's data is password protected and accessible only as prospective buyers meet certain performance requirements?
- Does the virtual data room software record which documents are reviewed and by whom?
- When documents are downloaded, does the system automatically record the party who executed the download?
- Do downloaded documents print with that user's name as a watermark so that, should the documents end up in other hands, there is an unambiguous link between the violator and the unauthorized user?

If you really want to know how sensitive an investment banker is to confidentiality concerns, speak to his or her past clients. Those who have been through the process can tell you exactly how well the investment banker performs in this highly sensitive area.

2. *Negotiating with one buyer is* faster than juggling multiple offers. This is true. A negotiated sale typically takes three months to complete, while the competitive auction takes six to twelve. But what's the rush? Unless there's a compelling reason (an owner's rapidly failing health, for example) to leave lots of cash on the table, I recommend taking the additional time to exploit the benefits of a competitive auction.

3. ***Negotiating with one buyer is* cheaper *than negotiating with multiple buyers.*** If you negotiate with one buyer, you can avoid paying the investment banker's monthly retainer and cut of the sale proceeds. If, however, you negotiate with that same buyer for months and the buyer decides to walk away from the deal, the money you paid your accountants and your attorneys for their assistance in completing the buyer's due diligence is gone. Poof. Their work and your cash are not transferable to a sale to another buyer as they would be if you were negotiating with multiple buyers. In a competitive auction, when one buyer leaves the table, you simply move another buyer into the departing buyer's chair.

4. ***Negotiating with one trusted buyer* increases the probability *that the deal will close.*** Deals with one buyer can fail just as easily as those with multiple buyers. But in the negotiated sale process, there are no other buyers also interested in buying the company. When a buyer is "the only game in town," sellers speak, think, and act differently than they do when they are working with multiple buyers.

For example, in any transaction, buyers constantly make requests or raise issues of their own. Each issue requires a "yes" or "no" from the seller. "We need a $100,000 environmental study done on that back lot." "We aren't sure that Customer X is going to stay with us after closing, so we want to hold back *x* percent of the purchase price." "Here's a list of fifteen more items we require to continue our due diligence."

If you have only one buyer at the table, how much leverage do you really have? Can you rationally consider each issue without thinking, "Is this the 'no' that is going to break the deal?" And if your negative response does cause the buyer to walk, then what?

Then you go back to square one: waiting for another buyer to show up with an offer.

Once owners understand that many of their assumptions about negotiated sales (negotiating with one buyer) do not hold water, they are usually willing to engage in a conversation about the competitive auction process. But before describing that process, let's consider how owners can use information, rather than assumptions, to choose the sale strategy best tailored to their situations.

MAKING AN INFORMED CHOICE

One of my favorite books about deal making is *Negotiauctions: New Deal-making Strategies for a Competitive Marketplace,* by Guhan Subramanian. Perhaps it is a favorite and one I frequently recommend because Subramanian's findings from his research concerning mega-deals are consistent with my experience in the midsize marketplace—namely, that most deals are not pure negotiations or pure auctions but some combination of both.

Subramanian packs *Negotiauctions* with insightful analysis and inside information about mega-deals pulled from the headlines, but the part of Subramanian's theory that intersects with our discussion here is the description of the factors you can use to determine whether a negotiated sale or a competitive auction is the most appropriate vehicle to sell your company.

Subramanian identifies four primary factors (BASC) in a seller's choice between negotiating with one buyer and an auction involving several:

1. The profile of the potential **B**uyer
2. The **A**sset characteristic
3. The profile of the **S**eller
4. **C**ontextual factors

For a complete discussion of each of these factors, I suggest you read *Negotiauctions.*

I have added to these lists some other factors that I have found to be operational in the midmarket. Those items are marked with an asterisk in the lists that follow.

1. Profile of potential buyer
   a. The number of bidders that we can attract to the auction
   b. The degree of certainty about who these bidders might be
   c. The bidders' incentives to participate
   d. The distribution of valuations

As you recall, in the last step of the Proactive Sale Strategy we identify potential buyers. To do so, we perform an enormous amount of research and include a company on our prospective buyer list only if we think (1) it has an incentive to participate (see Chapter 7, "Leverage Your Company's Competitive Advantage") and (2) it is financially capable of paying our desired purchase price. (Note: Subramanian's definition of *incentive to participate* has to do with the number of alternatives a buyer has to a negotiated agreement. By leveraging a competitive advantage, we limit that number of alternatives.)

What we try to predict, but simply cannot know, is which potential buyer might pay the highest price. In my opinion, the competitive auction is the best way to flush out the high bidder.

Finally, if a seller has two wildly divergent valuations in hand, Subramanian argues that it is best to negotiate because an auction will likely leave lots of value on the table.

In a midmarket transaction, two very different valuations don't necessarily indicate the need for a negotiated sale. As long as there is no publicly traded company involved, I continue to negotiate with the high bidder while running a competitive auction for other prospective buyers. By doing so, I protect my client from the risks of negotiating with only one bidder and maximize the opportunity to close for the greatest amount of cash.

Similarly, if there is an opportunity for a midmarket seller to pursue the Outrageous Price, two vastly different offers do not necessarily indicate a preference for a negotiated sale. When one buyer offers significantly more than another, that buyer is telling us something critical, either about the value of the synergies it expects to exploit or about the level of discomfort the seller is causing it. If presented with two disparate bids, I'll continue the competitive auction to protect the seller but negotiate individually with the high bidder.

   2. Asset characteristic
       a. Ability to specify the underlying asset
       b. Potential for value creation
       c. Importance of relationship between buyer and seller
       d. Size*

When Subramanian talks about specifying the underlying asset, he's referring to the ability to define what is for sale. Usually, it is easier to define a commodity than a service that depends on relationships, although some companies work in such highly esoteric areas (specialized high-tech and biomedical research come to mind) that there are not enough bidders who understand the asset to hold a competitive auction. In these cases, we look for and negotiate with the best possible buyer.

In Subramanian's world, "potential for value creation" is the capacity a transaction has to increase value for both parties. Can you hear the echoes from Chapter 5 of why we limit our buyer search to strategic buyers? Strategic buyers are those who make acquisitions based on their projections of the target's performance under their ownership rather than on any set financial formula.

Those involved in mega-deals certainly consider the importance of their relationship with a potential buyer as a factor in their choice of negotiated sale or competitive auction, but the relationship factor can assume gargantuan importance to owners in the midmarket. If buyer and seller have a close relationship, this factor can trump all others.

To Subramanian's list of asset characteristics, I add size. In the world he studies, deals are a clash of titans. In the midmarket, we can engage in the Outrageous Price Process only if a seller is large enough to attract the attention of a much larger buyer.

3. Seller's profile
   a. Importance of speed
   b. Tolerance for risk
   c. Nonfinancial objectives* (continue culture, values, location in one community)
   d. Decision to sell to management or family members*
   e. Desire to pick among offers*
   f. Desire to maintain negotiating strength*
   g. Desire for money*

Subramanian identifies only two seller attributes as factors in a company's decision to sell via a negotiated sale or a competitive auction: importance of speed and tolerance for risk. While these factors do influence midsize sellers, I've observed that other factors significantly impact their decisions to pursue a negotiated sale or a competitive auction.

For example, in the midsize market, the decision to sell is usually made by one person, and that one person is often the founder of the company. That person can be acutely sensitive to family dynamics, as his or her decision to sell impacts not only longtime employees but also his or her children, spouse, in-laws, and/or grandchildren.

Other sellers have such a strong aversion to jumping through the hoops of one buyer that they'll choose the competitive auction to gain the ability to rein in or dismiss unreasonable buyers. They greatly value the ability to choose among offers.

Others see the competitive auction as the best possible way for them to maintain their negotiating strength. Especially in cases in which all the buyers at the table are professionals and all are much larger in size, the competitive auction gives sellers a better stronghold from which to negotiate.

There are owners who, after comparing the two sales strategies, determine that the competitive auction affords the best shot at the highest possible sale price. In all but a few cases, I believe these owners are correct.

    4. Contextual factors
       a. Need for secrecy
       b. Buyer's need for transparency

Finally, Subramanian identifies two contextual factors that influence a seller's choice of sales method. Subramanian argues that if news of a possible sale would "damage the very asset they are trying to sell," sellers should opt for a negotiated sale (p. 52).

Earlier in this chapter I described some of the many ways to maintain deal confidentiality, but no protection process is perfect. Maintaining confidentiality with one buyer *is easier* than doing so with several. But I would default to the negotiated sale process only if the damage a breach would cause to the company *is mortal*. Over the years, I've learned that (1) very few confidentiality breaches are fatal to the company and (2) most breaches can be traced to the seller. The temptation to talk about a pending deal is one some sellers simply cannot resist.

Auctions can be more transparent than negotiated sales and must be so in the world of publicly traded companies. Think of the process of securing a contract with a government entity: All prospective buyers (or contractors) receive the same information about the selling company at the same time. This same transparency is not required and is very rare in the midmarket.

Table 11.1 helps summarize how each factor might indicate the appropriate sales vehicle—the negotiated sale or the competitive auction.

THE COMPETITIVE AUCTION PATH

After considering the pros and cons of both sale methods, you, as the seller, make your choice. And, since you picked up this book to learn how to get an Outrageous Price for your company, let's assume that your choice is to pursue

Table 11-1. Negotiated sale and competitive auction.

Characteristic	Factor	Negotiated Sale	Competitive Auction
Potential Buyer Profile	Number of bidders	If low.	If high.
	Degree of certainty about who prospective bidders will be	If high and good offer is in hand.	If low, use auction to flush out high bidder.
	Bidders' incentives to participate		If high, use to get Outrageous Price.
	Distribution of valuations	If narrow, negotiated sale is possible.	If wide, auction yields true market answer.
Characteristic	**Factor**	**Negotiated Sale**	**Competitive Auction**
Asset Profile	Ability to specify the underlying asset	Is one person's opinion of value.	Helps to specify the asset.
	Potential for value creation		Brings only strategic buyers to table.
	Importance of relationship between buyer and seller	If high.	Relationships between buyer and seller harder to maintain.
	Size of seller's company	Too small to attract multiple buyers.	Sufficient mass to attract multiple buyers.
Characteristic	**Factor**	**Negotiated Sale**	**Competitive Auction**
Seller Profile	Importance of speed	3 months (Outrageous Price not possible).	6–12 months.
	Tolerance for risk	If low.	Better chance of closing due to seller's leverage.
	Nonfinancial objectives (continuity of culture, value, or location)	✓	
	Desire to sell to management or family members	✓	
	Desire to pick among offers		✓
	Desire for best possible price		✓

Characteristic	Factor	Negotiated Sale	Competitive Auction
Contextual Factors	Need for secrecy	If high.	If tolerable and investment banker knows how to manage.
	Importance of transparency to buyer		✓

the competitive auction. Even if you cannot go for the Outrageous Price (due to the absence of one or more of the Four Pillars), the competitive auction is the best way to reduce the risk of not closing and the best way of getting the highest possible price.

As the driver of this bus, how do you start the competitive auction?

Buyer List

We'll assume that, as part of the Proactive Sale Strategy, your investment banker has completed a list of potential buyers. He or she created that list with your input and from a number of sources, including trade association membership lists, data and analysis, media and Internet searches, and, you hope, extensive networking in your industry and others. That list likely includes both public and private companies, such as private equity groups, industry players, adjacencies (companies in industries adjacent to yours), and competitors.

You and your investment banker will cull that list to between 100 and 500 strategic and financial buyers. If you have interviewed investment banking firms or have previously sold a company, this number may seem extravagant to you. I considered it standard operating procedure until I received a call from a "database expert" offering (for a fee, of course) access to his list of "nearly 500 PEGs!" Over the years, my firm has poured thousands of dollars into developing a proprietary database of buyers that includes more than 4,000 PEGs and 22,000 of the principals who manage those PEGs. The database salesman did ask if I'd consider selling our list. I passed.

Deal Book

You or someone you designate in your organization will work closely with your investment banking firm to collect data about every aspect of your company so that the investment banker can create a deal book (and other marketing materials) that tells a compelling story about your company—without revealing its identity. "Data" in this case includes:

◆ Company history
  ◇ General location
  ◇ Geographic growth
  ◇ Growth in number of employees
  ◇ Size of plant
  ◇ Notable achievements

◆ Industry analysis
  ◇ Forecasts for seller's industry
  ◇ Trends in seller's industry
  ◇ Forecasts and trends in industries seller serves

◆ Company analysis
  ◇ Overview of company
  ◇ Makeup of customer base
  ◇ Marketing/sales tactics
  ◇ Product/service description
  ◇ Production/execution process
  ◇ Capabilities
  ◇ Analysis of competitors

◆ Management summary
  ◇ Short biographies of key personnel

◆ Financial analysis
  ◇ Summary income statement
  ◇ Balance sheet

◆ Opportunities for growth
  ◇ Highlights of each area that holds potential for future growth

◆ Competitive advantages
  ◇ Description of each

◆ Key facts
  ◇ Facility
  ◇ Corporate status
  ◇ Fiscal year-end
  ◇ Number of employees

◇   Owner's reason for sale
◇   Description of asset/stock or sale
◇   Statement of management's posttransaction plans

Investment Banker Approaching Potential Buyers

Using e-mail blasts, letters, and personal calls to potential buyers, your investment banker *generically describes* your company and offers recipients more information in return for signed nondisclosure agreements. A *generic description* is one that prevents prospective buyers from discovering the identity of your company. For example, we may situate a seller's company in a region of the country (e.g., the Northeast) rather than in its home state or, on rare occasions, place it in a different state altogether. If your company is the only (and therefore instantly recognizable) large-scale taxidermist in Hawaii, we may "relocate" the company to California. We abandon this type of ruse as early in the process as possible, but only after we have protected our sellers with signed nondisclosure agreements.

Protecting Confidential Information

We have discussed many of the techniques your investment banker can (and I argue, should) use to protect your company's identity up to this point. But the deal book in exchange for a nondisclosure agreement is not the end of the confidentiality process. Protecting confidentiality is an ongoing project.

✦   By releasing additional information only after the prospective buyer performs a certain task (that usually involves investing its cash into the process), we not only protect confidentiality but also measure the buyer's commitment to the process.

✦   By classifying information from least sensitive to most sensitive, we not only take time to evaluate each piece of information and how it might be used but can schedule its release early (for nonsensitive information) or later in the process.

I often compare this measured release of information to the dating process. Rarely does an individual tell a first date about her $200,000 unpaid student loan, or about his attachment to Mom's basement, or about her membership in the biggest crime family in town. All these warts are revealed before the wedding but probably not during the first few dates.

Appendix F is a template for a basic nondisclosure agreement that my firm uses with prospective buyers. We negotiate the specific terms of our NDAs with each and every buyer based on that buyer's history in the marketplace.

If, for example, I've dealt with a buyer who has acted with integrity in past transactions, the NDA it signs will protect the seller but not be as restrictive in scope as an NDA with a buyer with which we have no history. NDAs are also highly restrictive when the prospective buyer is a competitor of the seller.

We often spend a week to ten days negotiating the scope of the nondisclosure agreement. For example, the person who signs the NDA may want the luxury of handing off a document to a colleague in another cubicle to review. As written, that is not allowed. The signer may want to download documents to send to its law firm for review. Again, the NDA as currently written does not allow the signer to do this. In these cases, the guy in the cubicle next door or the law firm down the street must each sign a separate NDA.

Getting into the Starting Gates

Once buyers sign and return their nondisclosure agreements, your investment banker will answer buyer questions and motivate them to make their best possible offers.

I use this time to ask buyers questions that disclose their reasons for being interested in this transaction. "What does your company plan to do with the seller's company?" "What synergies are you hoping the transaction will create?" In the midmarket, we sometimes find that buyers who fumble their answers to my questions aren't serious buyers. Instead, they are out gathering competitive intelligence.

Once investment bankers have NDAs in hand and are comfortable that the potential buyers' interest justifies moving forward, they set the due date for all buyers' expressions of interest.

Expressions of Interest

A buyer's expression of interest contains its account of the transaction. It is a *nonbinding* description of:

- ◆ What the buyer proposes to buy (stock, assets, real estate, patents, etc.)
- ◆ The price the buyer is willing to pay
- ◆ The means (or terms) the buyer will use to pay the purchase price (usually some combination of cash, promissory note, and stock)
- ◆ The buyer's desired postclosing relationship with the seller

Investment Banker and Seller Review of Expressions of Interest

In a typical deal, we receive expressions of interest from fifteen or so candidates that are (or could be) in our ballpark. The seller and investment banker then sit down to determine which expressions of interest align the seller's objectives with the buyers' offers and strategize how to persuade members of this group to improve their offers in their letters of intent.

Your investment banker communicates with these fifteen candidates to determine which are serious about pursuing the sale. In my conversations with candidates, I remind them that to submit a lowball offer at this point is to remove themselves from the process. Their offers must be competitive to progress to the next stage of the deal process. Typically, we'll choose as many as five finalists to invite to the management presentations.

Management Presentations

Typically, I invite the best five candidates to attend separate, carefully scripted, and time-limited management presentations.

The purpose of the management presentation is to provide the opportunity for the buyer to kick the selling company's tires while maintaining the seller's confidentiality. The buyer wants to meet the seller and see the seller's company. While meeting the seller is possible, seeing the company presents sellers with serious concerns. At this stage of the game, sellers do not want their employees to know that they are even remotely considering a sale. So I have conducted site visits after business hours and on weekends. In some situations, we have physically covered machinery or inventory that might give the buyer information that could hurt the seller if the deal were to collapse.

The seller's goal for these meetings is to provide enough—and usually more sensitive—information to make the buyer comfortable in raising the price it will offer in its letter of intent. We provide to the buyer a forty- to fifty-slide PowerPoint presentation that contains more detailed (and sensitive) analysis of the selling company. That presentation also helps the seller and his or her management team to prepare their answers to the buyer's questions. It describes all aspects of the company, and it controls the conversation in the room.

Attending these meetings are the buyer and its representatives, the seller/ owner and his or her management team, and the investment banker. I moderate the meeting, while the owner and management team answer the buyer's questions.

We schedule these half-day meetings over the course of one week in a hotel conference room. In most cases, meetings occur in the seller's hometown, but if the seller operates from a small town, we move the meetings to a location where the seller is not as well known.

Again, the purpose of the meetings, the PowerPoint presentation, and everything we've done to this point is to make prospective buyers comfortable enough to make their best offers in their letters of intent.

Letters of Intent

Up to this point, sellers and buyers have presented themselves in the best possible light. Sellers have highlighted their best assets, and serious buyers have done what they can to assure the seller that they are serious contenders who can close the deal. It is time for the courting process to end and for each party to state its intentions.

In the M&A world, buyers state their intentions to sellers in partially binding letters of intent (LOIs). Just as an engagement ring is not a wedding ring, a letter of intent is not a binding purchase contract, so the transaction cannot be consummated based on its terms. These letters do, however, refine the numbers that have been tossed around up to this point and contain a sketch of the terms of the deal.

Before jumping into the highlights of the letter of intent, know that there is no standard letter. In fact, in some transactions there's no letter of intent at all! Letters of intent can be one page or ten pages, usually depending upon the experience and/or contentiousness of the two parties. Length may also be a function of the investment banker's intuition. If your investment banker has reason to suspect that an issue has the potential to wreck the deal, he or she negotiates the most comprehensive letter of intent possible.

For example, if I suspect that a buyer is going to be particularly prickly about due diligence protocol or a sensitive issue related to one or more representations or warranties, I negotiate that issue in the letter of intent so that the parties reach an agreement before the letter is signed and the stop-shop agreement takes effect. It is better for sellers that deals blow up at this point rather than after they've taken their companies off the market and invested thousands of dollars (and megawatts of emotional energy) into due diligence.

◆ **The *what* of the deal.** While this may sound too obvious to mention, you might be surprised at the number of sellers who are stunned to learn that a buyer is purchasing only assets, or only stock, or only a portion of its inventory, or that the buyer is not assuming certain liabilities. The *what* of the deal is the detailed description of what is being purchased.

◆ **Purchase price.** If accepted, the buyer's offer (usually expressed as a formula rather than a specific dollar amount) in this letter stands, unless it is "adjusted" according to other terms in the contract. Usually, the formula relates to the seller's asset value, the seller's expected earnings, or a blend of the two. Sellers want to allow as few adjustments as possible, while buyers want as much flexibility as possible. Buyers will seek to adjust the purchase price to account for any change in earnings, working capital, or net worth between the date of the letter of intent and the closing.

◆ **Confidentiality.** It is not yet time to announce the planned marriage. Letters of intent should reiterate that nondisclosure agreements remain in place.

◆ **Breakdown of purchase price.** Purchases are generally made in some combination of cash, promissory notes, and earnouts. The buyer sets its desired allocation, but these percentages are subject to vigorous negotiation. Assuming there is a promise to pay a portion of the purchase price on future dates, the letter specifies the terms of the promissory note, but, again, all terms are open for negotiation.

◆ **Employment agreement for the seller (if any).** In traditional sales (non-Outrageous), buyers usually require sellers to stay with the company for a negotiated period of time. The length of time depends on the seller's preferences and the buyer's assessment of the strength of the company's other managers.

In Outrageous Sales, we find that buyers rarely require or even ask sellers to remain with the company after closing. Especially if the seller has caused the buyer significant pain, the buyer wants the seller gone, baby, gone.

If, however, the synergies that the buyer expects from the transaction are seller-based (such as the seller's great relationships with customers or specific know-how that exists only in the seller's head), the buyer will want to keep the seller on board for the length of time it believes it will take to transfer those relationships or that knowledge to someone else in the new company.

◆ **Working capital adjustments.** *Working capital* is defined as the excess of current assets less current liabilities. In a business, the amount of working capital fluctuates daily as assets (typically cash, accounts receivable, and inventory) and liabilities (accounts payable, accruals, taxes, wages, and salaries payable) change. In its letter of intent, the buyer makes an assumption of the seller's working capital but will conduct a review of all its components on the day of closing. Based on its closing date valuation, the buyer will make a corresponding adjustment to the purchase price. Pretty simple, right?

Well, since a business is not a fixed asset, agreeing on how to calculate the amount of working capital the seller is leaving behind is almost always a subject of contention at the end of the deal and postclosing. Agreeing to a formula is tricky because it attempts to calculate and assign a value to some component of the business—inventory, accounts receivable, etc.—at the time the deal is consummated. For example, if the item is accounts receivable, will a ninety-one-day receivable be included in the calculation? If so, will it be included at its full dollar amount or at a discounted amount?

Using the same set of numbers, you and I could arrive at two very different adjustments depending on what accounting protocol we use.

There are two ways to minimize conflict in this area. First, sellers should scrub their books clean prior to entering the marketplace. Remove any personal expenses, such as salaries to children, loans to employees, or ownership of recreational vehicles. Remove the deadwood from the company's accounts receivable either by collecting or writing them off. Clean books make buyers more comfortable, and comfortable buyers move through due diligence more quickly.

The second way to minimize postclosing drama is to define, as clearly as possible, the methodologies for calculating assets and liabilities. Your investment banker and accountant will work with you to create the most favorable formulas possible.

◆ **Breakup fee**. Today we see breakup fees in letters of intent for larger deals as buyers seek to cover the substantial expense that they incur in due diligence. Sellers are not averse to breakup fees because they want buyers—especially in a tight credit environment—to demonstrate their intent to close deals.

◆ **Representations and warranties**. Representations and warranties are the icing on the buyer's due diligence cake. These are the statements of fact sellers make to buyers to assure buyers that every little thing is on the up-and-up. No matter how thorough, buyers are never convinced that their due diligence has unearthed every possible fault. So they expect sellers to warrant that they have complied with every tax law, permitting or governmental requirement, and contractual or implied obligation of every conceivable kind. What due diligence may have missed, the representations and warranties cover—and provide the buyer recourse should any fact be found inaccurate.

Not surprisingly, representations and warranties are often the subject of the fiercest and most protracted negotiations.

In a sense, representations and warranties work much like an insurance policy. First, there are exclusions, the most common of which are tax and environmental issues. The seller is held responsible for any environmental violation that occurred on its watch in perpetuity. Second, in the representations and warranties there's a "basket" that works much likes a deductible. The seller pays the buyer only for damages that exceed the basket amount. Finally, there's a lifetime limit, or cap, on the amount a seller could be liable to pay a buyer. As you might expect, buyers and sellers spend a great deal of time negotiating the exclusions, baskets, and caps.

The seller's primary goal in negotiating these issues is to limit its exposure to those items or issues *it has knowledge of.* For example, a seller will want to change "Seller warrants that there are no actions, suits, claims, investigations, or legal, administrative, or arbitration proceedings pending or threatened against it" to "Seller warrants that, *to its knowledge,* there are no actions, suits, claims, investigations, or legal, administrative, or arbitration proceedings pending or threatened against it." One clause can make a world of difference.

◆ **Financing sources and contingencies**. As a seller, you want to limit the opportunities for the buyer to walk away from the deal due to an inability to secure financing. Your investment banker should review the buyer's commitment letter from its source of financing and determine how creditworthy the lender is. Once you sign the letter of intent, your company is off the auction block, so you want your investment banker to determine the likelihood that the buyer's financing will remain secure through closing before you sign the LOI.

Stop-Shop Agreement

The letter of intent contains the stop-shop agreement, an exclusivity period during which the seller agrees to cease discussions with any current or future potential buyers. This period can last between 30 and 120 days and takes effect as soon as the seller signs the LOI. No matter how long the exclusivity period lasts, reentering the marketplace puts sellers at a huge disadvantage. Potential buyers view these companies as tainted goods. They know that an interested buyer vanished and, to figure out why, will dissect every piece of information that sellers disclose.

The stop-shop agreement is not, however, a buyer's blank check to take its own sweet time in conducting due diligence and contract negotiations. To protect sellers, we limit the duration of the agreement (usually to between sixty and ninety days) and build into it two important limits on the buyer's activities. The first is an unambiguous statement that if the buyer attempts to retrade or whittle away at the purchase price established in the LOI, the stop-shop evaporates. (See Chapter 3 for a description of retrading.)

The second constraint on a buyer's behavior that we include in the stop-shop agreement is a series of hurdle dates. The buyer must clear each hurdle successfully, or the stop-shop agreement ceases. For example, we set dates by which the buyer must provide a first draft of the purchase contract, finalize the purchase contract, secure financing commitments, gain board of director approval for the transaction (if applicable), and complete any due diligence.

A buyer's compliance with hurdle dates maintains deal momentum, demonstrates its interest in the transaction, and gives the seller some comfort that if the buyer does walk from the deal it does so quickly rather than after a protracted period of time.

If you are one of the few sellers lucky enough to have multiple buyers at the table keenly interested in consummating the transaction, your investment banker may be able to eliminate the stop-shop agreement from the letter of intent. But deleting a stop-shop—even in Outrageous Sales—is rare simply because buyers will not devote time or money to negotiations with a seller who continues to actively court other suitors.

Due Diligence

Once the seller signs a buyer's letter of intent, the buyer can begin its due diligence. We described presale due diligence in detail in Chapter 3, but keep in mind that that was just the warm-up. In *presale* due diligence, the seller's advisers make their best guess of what documents the buyer will want to examine. In due diligence, the buyer's advisers are driving the process. In the buyer's due diligence, the level of detail and the scope of the items buyers now routinely request have risen to a level we've never before experienced. (See Appendix B and Appendix C.)

It is worth reiterating here that until you have gone through the due diligence process, you will likely be stunned and frustrated by it. If sellers lose their cool anytime during the sale process, the meltdown will likely occur during the buyer's due diligence. As buyers expect sellers to produce thousands of pages of data (3,000 to 5,000 pages is not unusual), most sellers feel justifiably overwhelmed.

Negotiating the Definitive Purchase Agreement

In a traditional (non–Outrageous Sale), I prefer that the seller's investment banker, with the assistance of the seller's attorney, negotiate the definitive purchase agreement. I don't feel as strongly about who drafts the agreement—buyer's attorney or seller's attorney—as I do about who leads the contract negotiations. In the pursuit of an Outrageous Price, it is imperative that the investment banker who has created the strategy lead the negotiations.

You may recall that in the Outrageous Price Process, every participant plays a carefully scripted role. Those roles continue until the curtain falls at closing—not a minute before. So it makes sense that the investment banker who created the scripts keeps his or her finger on the pulse of the deal.

There are a number of books that detail each section of a definitive purchase agreement, so, rather than recycle that material, let me share a few insights about the relationship between the letter of intent and the definitive purchase agreement.

♦ **Language and terms.** Overall, the language and terms of the definitive purchase agreement mirror those contained in the letter of intent. Since letters of intent vary greatly in length and level of detail, so too do the final contracts.

As mentioned earlier, the variations in letters of intent are primarily due to buyer and seller traits but can also reflect the inexperience of one of the parties' attorneys. When an attorney quibbles over every word because he or she is not experienced in transactions, the entire deal is in jeopardy.

There may also be numerous changes between the two documents if the seller or the company is not prepared for the sale process. I devoted an entire chapter of this book to presale due diligence for the simple reason that if a seller is emotionally unprepared or the company is practically unprepared for this process, the probability of the deal running off the tracks—permanently—increases dramatically. And it is during these definitive agreement negotiations that the train wreck usually occurs.

The first train wreck happens when the seller—having devoted every ounce of patience, perseverance, and determination to responding to the buyer's numerous due diligence requests—is too emotionally drained to make the 452nd decision in the contract negotiation phase. (I suggest you read *Willpower: Rediscovering the Greatest Human Strength*, by John Tierney and Roy F. Baumeister, for a complete discussion of this phenomenon or review the description of deal fatigue in Chapter 9.)

The second train wreck occurs when the buyer, as it combs through the thousands of pages that the seller has turned over during due diligence, finds something that—if it does not cause the buyer to rescind its offer—causes it to change drastically the terms of the deal.

◆ **Purchase price.** There should be no difference between the purchase price stated in the letter of intent and the one in the definitive purchase agreement unless the buyer uncovers something during its due diligence process.

◆ **Seller attitude.** It is worth repeating here that the seller who can maintain a devil-may-care-if-this-deal-closes-but-I-don't attitude has the best chance of making it to the closing table.

Closing

Imagine for a moment (or perhaps you already have) that you and your team (attorney, spouse, and investment banker) and the buyer and its team sit in a top-floor conference room. Floor-to-ceiling windows reveal the world at your feet—exactly how you feel as the ice melts in the champagne bucket and all parties chat politely as you and the buyer sign contracts and the buyer finally hands you *the check*.

A lovely but nostalgic scene, to be sure, but not one that bears much resemblance to today's closings. Well, your attorney may invite you to his or her penthouse conference room and spring for a bottle of champagne, but more likely you will be in your investment banker's office with your banker, who will let you know when the buyer's wired funds are received.

With that piece of good news, you imagine that you walk out of that closing with the weight of the world lifted from your shoulders. For the first time in years, you are free from financial worry.

Again, that's a great dream, and parts of it are true. Without drenching your parade, let me remind you that sellers are forever subject to a few of the warranties and representations made in the definitive purchase agreement and are subject to the bulk of them until the indemnification period expires. Remember those postclosing adjustments (discussed in Chapter 3) that reconcile the difference between your assumptions of value and the actual values on the date of closing? Those still need to be made.

Some sellers return to work for a new owner the day after closing. For others, the receipt of the entire purchase price is subject to the earnouts they negotiated because they wanted to include (and the buyer resisted) the value of the company's projected earnings in the sale price. If the growth the seller expected happens, the buyer pays. If that growth fails to occur, the buyer makes no payment.

Depending upon the exact terms of the purchase contract, I suggest that sellers imagine a moment eighteen to twenty-four months after the closing. All the postclosing adjustments have been made. Sellers have satisfied the terms of their employment agreements with their buyers. The period on any earnouts has expired, as has the indemnification period during which sellers can be held to the majority of representations and warranties. That image is not as captivating as handshakes and backslaps over sips of iced champagne, but it is the moment that sellers can finally exhale.

12

Wrap-Up

This book presents two challenges to every business owner:

- ◆ Can you sell your business?
- ◆ Can you sell it for an Outrageous Price?

When the temperature of the M&A market is between tepid and chilly, business owners easily fall into a self-defeating belief that in the absence of a "hot" market, their companies can't sell for even an acceptable price. If, after reading this book, you recognize that the temperature of the marketplace has little to do with the saleability and desirability of your company, I've done my job.

Getting a great price, or even an Outrageous Price, for your company is not a function of being in the right place at the right time—although let's never discount the value of serendipity! Getting a great price for a company is the product of preparation, analysis, and carefully executed strategy.

Preparation

There is no way to overstate the importance of laying a solid and strong foundation for a sale to a third party. The two best actions you can take to construct that foundation are to complete a Sale Readiness Assessment (see Appendix A) and engage in a vigorous a presale due diligence process (Chapter 3).

Analysis

Business owners who would never put a product or service on the market without significant planning and market analysis of how the product/service compares with similar ones will put their companies on the market without that same level of analysis. When I see this, I'm left scratching my head. How will these owners sell their companies when they really don't know what they are selling or how their companies differ from their competitors?

To persuade a buyer to pay two times as much as what it would pay for a similar company (the point of the Outrageous Price Process), we must do more than prepare a company. We must determine if the owner and his or her advisers have what it takes to complete the process. For an owner/seller, "what it takes" includes the intestinal fortitude to withstand the dives, bumps, and starts and stops that characterize the sale process. In addition, sellers must be able to trust their investment banker's ability to manage all the facets of the process. Finally, sellers must be able to assume—or at least maintain a convincing facade of—an "I don't care if I sell or not" attitude.

Even the smoothest sale process is no place for the weak of heart. The brinksmanship inherent to the Outrageous Price Process, however, takes a degree of self-control and self-discipline that some owners simply can't achieve.

Just as owners need to know whether they have what it takes to succeed in the Outrageous Price Process, they need to check the expertise and experience of their advisers. Many, if not most, investment bankers have no clue about how to execute the Outrageous Price Process. I urge future sellers to do their homework before hiring an adviser. You can use Appendix G to help you probe the experience of an investment banker, or you can hand him or her a copy of this book and meet for lunch a week later to discuss it.

Finally, it is worth your time (and money) to know the buyers that are actively acquiring companies like yours. While you will know some of the players, I hope you'll pick the brain of your investment banker to identify many others you may not have considered. Refer to Chapter 5 for types of buyers and how to locate them.

Strategy

Once you've laid the foundation for saleability, analyzed the strengths of your company, yourself, and your investment banker, and identified buyers in the marketplace, you—and only you—decide whether to pursue the Outrageous Price Process. But before you embark, I suggest that you ask your investment banker about the strategy he or she plans to use to entice and excite a buyer.

Buyers don't simply offer sellers Outrageous Prices on silver trays. Outrageous Buyers are professionals who use every trick in the book to chisel away at a sale price. To convince them that buying your company will eliminate a source of pain or cause it tremendous gain takes a carefully planned, yet responsive, strategy. No one can predict every action that a buyer might take, so I recommend that you hire the most creative investment banker you can find. I suggest you review Chapter 7 for examples of how several of my clients and I have executed strategies to achieve Outrageous Prices.

I contend that the process I've described in this book is the best possible way for owners/sellers to receive great, if not Outrageous, prices, for their companies. That said, the Outrageous Price Process is predictive. While it puts owners/sellers in control of as many variables as possible, it cannot control the wildest card in the deck: the temperament of the targeted buyer. The Outrageous Price Process sets a lovely table full of enticing dishes specially prepared and designed for the tastes of a particular buyer, but it cannot force that buyer to tuck in its napkin, relish the food, and order seconds. No sale process can do that.

But what the Outrageous Sale Process can do far outperforms every other sale strategy. It fully prepares a company and its owner for the marketplace. It identifies a company's competitive advantage as well as the obvious and not-so-obvious buyers in the buyer pool. It matches the strengths of the seller to the strength or weakness of a particular buyer and creates a strategy to show a buyer how much it will gain from an acquisition or the pain it will experience if it fails to make the acquisition.

Ultimately, the Outrageous Price Process is the one sale strategy that offers business owners their best shot at achieving their ultimate goal: selling an ordinary company for an Outrageous Price.

A

Sale Readiness Assessment

[This is the Sales Readiness Assessment that my company sends to potential clients.]

❖

To help us determine how prepared you and your company are for a possible sale and the assets your company can provide a buyer, please complete this Sale Readiness Assessment. If you do not understand what a question means or, more likely, want to provide us additional or clarifying information, please so indicate by checking the box marked "Ask me." Please return this assessment to us so we can meet with you to review your answers and ask additional questions.

❖ ❖

PART I: YOUR EXIT GOALS

	Comment	Ask Me
1. What are the characteristics of your "ideal" sale in terms of:		
1a. Price		
1b. Your role after the sale		
1c. Postacquisition role for your employees		
1d. Potential reorganization of the company		
1e. Optimal personal tax ramifications		
2. Is there a party (or parties) that you will not consider as a buyer?		

PART II: EXIT STRATEGY AWARENESS

	Yes	No	Comment	Ask Me
1. Do all owners agree with the "ideal" sale as outlined above?				
1a. If not, what are the differences?	N/A	N/A		
2. Is your board of directors aware of your exit strategy?				
2a. If so, do its members agree with your exit strategy?				
3. Is senior management aware of your exit strategy?				
3a. If so, do all senior managers agree with your exit strategy?				
4. Are key employees aware of your exit strategy?				
4a. If so, do all key employees agree with your exit strategy?				

PART III: FAMILY BUSINESS CONSIDERATIONS

	Yes	No	Comment	Ask Me
1. How will a transfer to a third party affect your:	N/A	N/A		
1a. Spouse?	→	→		
1b. Ex-spouse?	→	→		
1c. In-laws?	→	→		
1d. Business-active children?	→	→		
1e. Non-business-active children?	→	→		
2. Have you discussed your ideal sale plan with your:	N/A	N/A		
2a. Spouse?				
2b. Ex-spouse?				
2c. In-laws?				
2d. Business-active children?				
2e. Non-business-active children?				

PART III: FAMILY BUSINESS CONSIDERATIONS

	Yes	No	Comment	Ask Me
3. Do you have a succession plan for your company?				
3a. If so, is that plan in writing?				
4. Does any member of your family expect to succeed you in ownership?				

PART IV: YOUR COMPANY'S ADVISERS

	Yes	No	Comment	Ask Me
1. Is your relationship with your bank or primary lender:	N/A	N/A		
1a. Proactive?				
1b. On a need-to-know basis?				
1c. Somewhere in between?				
2. Do you work with a law firm skilled in transaction law?				
2a. If so, has this firm performed a legal audit of your company?				
3. Do you work with a CPA firm skilled in transactions?				
3a. If so, has this firm talked to you about strategies to minimize corporate and personal tax liability upon sale?				

PART V: YOUR COMPANY

A. Pricing

	Yes	No	Comment	Ask Me
1. Do you have a higher or lower price point than your competitors for your most profitable product/service?				
2. Do you engage in promotional pricing?				
2a. If so, what is your strategy?	N/A	N/A		

B. Costs

	Yes	No	Comment	Ask Me
1. Do you have a robust process in place to track your costs?				
2. Have you taken steps to reduce supply chain costs?				
3. Are you as effective as you'd like to be in negotiating the price of your raw materials?				
4. Do you effectively minimize your cost drivers?				

B. Costs

	Yes	No	Comment	Ask Me
5. Have you taken steps to ensure a lean production process?				
6. How have you improved your inventory management and capacity utilization rate?				
7. Does your company enjoy any economies of scale?				
7a. If it could do so, how would it be more profitable?	N/A	N/A		

C. People

	Yes	No	Comment	Ask Me
1. Do you follow a set strategy to attract and select employees?				
2. Do you know why your employees work for you?				
3. Is your management team both experienced and diversely talented?				
4. Have you/your company/your employees won any awards? Recognitions?				
5. Is your product development team different from your competitors'?				
5a. How?	N/A	N/A		
6. Do your employees affect your customers' purchase decisions?				
7. Does meeting your customers' needs depend on high-intellect or highly skilled employees?				
8. Do the salaries, benefits, and working conditions of your employees meet "industry standard"?				

D. Sales/Communications/Marketing

	Yes	No	Comment	Ask Me
1. Does your company have a written marketing plan?				
1a. Do you measure its results?				
1b. If so, have you communicated it to your employees?				
2. What is your company's market share in your industry?	N/A	N/A		
2a. Is its share increasing?				
2b. Is its share decreasing?				
2c. Is its share constant?				
2d. If your company's market share is changing, do you know why?				
3. Has your company's image/brand recognition changed over the years?				
4. Does your company have a written sales plan?				
4a. Do you measure its results?				

D. Sales/Communications/Marketing

	Yes	No	Comment	Ask Me
4b. Have you communicated it to your employees?				
5. Does your sales team communicate the strengths of your product/service?				
6. Can you influence demand for your product/service?				
7. Are your company's distribution channels the same as your competitors'?				
7a. If not, how are they different, better, or worse?	N/A	N/A		

E. Technology

	Yes	No	Comment	Ask Me
1. Does your company have a technological advantage over its competitors?				
2. What steps do you take to improve/update your technical capabilities?	N/A	N/A		
3. Are rights to all technology registered to the company?				
3a. Are those rights current?				
3b. Are those rights transferable to a new owner?				

F. Business Strategy/Business Model

	Yes	No	Comment	Ask Me
1. Do you have a business model?				
2. Do you have a written business plan?				
2a. Is the plan up-to-date?				
2b. Do you use it to make decisions?				
3. Do you have a vision for your company's future?				
3a. Do you share that vision with your employees?				
4. How much of the information necessary to run the company, maintain its customer base, develop new products, or generate new sales leads is dependent on you?	N/A	N/A		

G. Industry

	Yes	No	Comment	Ask Me
1. How do companies in your industry make money?	N/A	N/A		
2. In what ways is your industry changing?	N/A	N/A		
2a. What have you done to keep pace with changes?	N/A	N/A		
2b. How successful have those actions been?	N/A	N/A		

G. Industry

	Yes	No	Comment	Ask Me
3. Are there threats to your company:	N/A	N/A		
3a. Currently?				
3b. In the short term?				
3c. In the long term?				
4. Are there governmental or licensing regulations that apply to your company or industry?				
4a. If so, how robust is your compliance with these regulations or requirements?	N/A	N/A		

H. Customers

	Yes	No	Comment	Ask Me
1. Who are your customers?	N/A	N/A		
2. Do you know why your customers buy from you instead of from your competitors?				
3. Do you know why your customers left their previous vendor/ service provider?				
4. Are you effective in increasing your customers' profits?				
4a. Do you know how much you save them?				
5. Are your current customers your target market?				
6. How do you find out what customers need?	N/A	N/A		
7. What is your customer retention rate?	N/A	N/A		
8. Do you have data indicating how customers rate your customer service?				
9. What percentage of your business comes from referrals?	N/A	N/A	_ percent	
10. Does one (or several) customer account for a significant percentage of the company's sales?				

I. Systems

	Yes	No	Comment	Ask Me
1. Are your systems sophisticated and complete enough to show how well your company is managed?				
2. Does your company have:	N/A	N/A		
2a. Audited financial statements?				
2b. Reviewed financial statements?				

I. Systems

	Yes	No	Comment	Ask Me
2c. Compiled financial statements?				
2d. Budget projections and comparisons?				
3. Do you have systems in place to reduce the risk of litigation from customers, suppliers, and vendors?				
3a. Do you use contracts to reduce risk with these parties?				
3b. Do these contracts meet "industry standard"?				
3c. Can these contracts be assigned?				

PART VI: YOUR COMPANY'S COMPETITORS

	Yes	No	Comment	Ask Me
1. Who are your company's competitors?	N/A	N/A		
2. Have you ever taken advantage of a competitor's mistake or weakness?				
2a. If not, have you ever perceived the opportunity but for some reason did not act?				
2b. What prevented you from taking action?	N/A	N/A		
3. Is there a competitor (or several) who would like to see your company out of business?				
3a. Why?	N/A	N/A		
4. How do your competitors make money?	N/A	N/A		
5. Have you compared your company's metrics to industry standards?				
5a. If so, how does your company compare?	N/A	N/A		

PART VII: POTENTIAL BUYERS

	Yes	No	Comment	Ask Me
1. Can you list competitors who might (under the right conditions) be interested in purchasing your company?				
2. Are there customers, vendors, or others outside your industry that might be interested in buying your company?				
3. Do you have contacts in any of these organizations?				
4. Do you have relationships or linkages (sit on each other's boards) with potential buyers?				

PART VIII: CURRENT ACQUISITION ACTIVITY

	Yes	No	Comment	Ask Me
1. Are there specific valuation issues that are unique to your industry or to recent industry transactions?				
2. What is the current volume of deal activity in your industry?	N/A	N/A		
3. Do you know how much buyers making recent acquisitions in your marketplace are paying?				
4. Do you know if these buyers are paying in all cash or some combination of cash and equity?				
5. Do you know what size acquisitions buyers are making?				
6. Do you know why buyers are making these acquisitions?				

PART IX: YOUR COMPANY'S COMPETITIVE ADVANTAGE

	Yes	No	Comment	Ask Me
1. Do you currently differentiate your company from competitors?				
1a. Based on price?				
1b. Based on quality?				
1c. Based on service?				
2. Are you searching for or developing a new competitive advantage?				
3. Can your product/service be easily replicated or substituted?				
4. Are there limits to your company's scalability, such as legislative/regulatory issues or requirements for a good infrastructure or highly educated workforce?				
5. Why do you think a buyer would want to purchase your company?	N/A	N/A		
6. How could you better position your company to appeal to a buyer?	N/A	N/A		

Legal and Financial Due Diligence List

1. Legal Considerations

- Contracts with manufacturers, distributors, customers, vendors, and suppliers
- Sales, supply, service, and maintenance agreements
- Government contracts
- Express warranties and disclaimers of warranties (last five years)
- Performance or custom bonds
- Powers of attorney
- Agreements restricting the conduct of the company or its business
- Letters of intent
- Personal property leases
- Standard company business forms
- Indemnification agreements

2. Corporate Organization

- ◆ Articles of incorporation
- ◆ Bylaws
- ◆ Stock certificates and stock book
- ◆ Stock transfer ledgers for the company
- ◆ List of board of directors
  - ◇ Include brief description of current duties and current compensation
- ◆ Minutes of board of directors' meetings
- ◆ Minutes of shareholder meetings
- ◆ Minutes of any committee meetings
- ◆ List of shareholders (break out on a fully diluted basis, including options, warrants, etc.)
- ◆ List of shareholder responsibilities
- ◆ Copies of any shareholder agreements
- ◆ List of current officers
  - ◇ Include brief description of current duties and current compensation
- ◆ List of subsidiaries or related companies
- ◆ List of all partnerships, joint ventures, or affiliates
- ◆ Business plan (last two years)
- ◆ List of states in which the company is qualified to transact business and all certificates of authority
  - ◇ Provide good standing certificates
- ◆ Copies of all legal opinions prepared for the company relating to its organization and/or its business within the last five years
- ◆ Copies of all voting trust agreements and other voting agreements

3. Financial Statements and Reports

- ◆ Historical year-end financial statements (audited, CPA-prepared, and internally generated for last three fiscal years)
- ◆ Monthly (interim) unaudited financial statements for current fiscal year
- ◆ Copies of all management letters and special reports from auditors (and responses thereto)

- Schedule of all bank accounts, certificates of deposit, and safe deposit boxes
  ◇ Address
  ◇ Individual authorized to sign on account
- General ledger, sales journals, and cash receipts journal for last fiscal year
- Breakdown of officers' and others' salaries as a component of general and administrative expenses (analysis of officer/shareholder benefits—compensation, benefits, and perks for past three years and year-to-date comparable to the same time period during prior fiscal year)
- Description of accounting policies and changes thereto
- Documentation of the company's procedures/controls
- Schedule of current year's customer revenues vs. current year's budgeted revenues
- List of liabilities not reflected on interim financial statements
  ◇ Include material or potentially material contingent liabilities
- Description of any material damage, destruction, or loss (whether or not covered by insurance) suffered in past five years
- List of capital expenditures for the past three fiscal years and year-to-date identifying whether the expenditure was for maintenance or to support growth of the company
- Projections, forecasts, and budgets (last two years)
- Projections and/or budgets for current and next two years:
  ◇ Include capital expenditure forecast
  ◇ Break down growth between (i) organic within existing accounts or (ii) related to new accounts
  ◇ Include revenue, unit, and gross margin assumptions for each customer/channel as applicable
- Schedule of recently introduced new products and revenue and unit assumptions for current and next three years
- Schedule of planned new product introductions and revenue and unit assumptions for current and next three years
- List of assets and liabilities on the balance sheet that will not be sold with the company (e.g., personal vehicle)
- List of tax asset detail showing all fixed assets and depreciation

- Breakdown of revenues for each entity over past three years
  - ◇ By type of customer
  - ◇ By product category
  - ◇ By geography
  - ◇ By independent sales rep/word of mouth/employees/etc.
- Accounts payable aging and reconciliation to general ledger (most recent month-end that ties to balance sheet)
- Long-term liabilities and commitments (other than notes, payable, and inventory commitments exceeding six months)
  - ◇ List of banking and credit activities
  - ◇ Agreements related to indebtedness
  - ◇ List of guarantees or indemnification agreements
  - ◇ Letters of credit
  - ◇ Revolving credit agreements
  - ◇ Lease-purchase agreements
  - ◇ Equity purchase agreements
  - ◇ List of accrued liabilities and reconciliation to general ledger
  - ◇ Schedule of notes and loans payable
- Other financial information will be requested separately.

4. Tax

- Income tax returns for past five years:
  - ◇ Federal
  - ◇ State/local
- Franchise, sales property, and excise tax returns for all open years, including:
  - ◇ Tax elections
  - ◇ Election to be taxed as an S corporation
- Sales and use tax returns for past five years
- Payroll and unemployment tax returns for past five years
- All IRS or state revenue department correspondence for past five years
- Notices or proposed adjustments received from federal, state, local, or foreign authorities regarding returns, deficiency claims with regard to income, sales, property, or other taxes

- Description of tax accounting and depreciation methods (including any changes)
- Copies of any extension of the statute of limitations for any tax years for any tax

5. Agreements, Commitments, and Understandings (Verbal and Written)

- Shareholder agreements
- Voting agreements
- Agreements, arrangements, or understandings by the company or its shareholders to issue, purchase, or sell any securities of the company
- List of written consents related to the company
- List of any sale or grant of any option, warrant, right of first refusal, purchase plan, or other right to purchase capital stock, including copies of any agreements or documents related thereto
- All agreements, orders, or commitments for the purchase or lease of capital equipment, components, assemblies, supplies, inventories, or finished goods in excess of $10,000 per any one agreement, order, or commitment
- All agreements or orders of commitments for the sale of products or assets in excess of $10,000 for any one agreement, order, or commitment
- All other agreements, contracts, or commitments involving the payment or receipt of more than $10,000 in any individual case, including copies of all agreements relating to the borrowing of money or extension of credit, including those with affiliates, directors or officers, or other employees of the company
- Copies of all sales agency or representative, manufacturer representative, distributorship, and franchise agreements
- Copies of all requirement, output, and supply contracts
- Copies of all partnership or joint venture agreements
- All agreements, contracts, or commitments not entered into in the ordinary course of business
- All product or service warranties extended to customers of the company, including the warranty claims history with respect thereto

◆ A list of all transactions, and copies of all agreements, between the company and any subsidiary or between the company and any of its directors, officers, or other affiliated parties (or members of their immediate families, which includes spouses, parents, children, siblings, mothers, fathers, and all in-laws)

6. Consents, Authorizations, and Approvals Necessary to Complete the Transaction

◆ Copies of any offering or disclosure documents prepared with respect to the sale of the company

◆ All agreements, contracts, or commitments that are subject to suspension, revocation, cancellation, modification, or termination by, or that require notice to or consent of, any third party upon a change of control of the company

◆ Lists and copies of all permits, licenses, and governmental or regulatory franchises and indication of any permit, license, or franchise that is subject to suspension, revocation, cancellation, or modification, whether upon a change of control of the company or otherwise

7. Employment

◆ List of all employees:
  ◇ Name
  ◇ Classification
  ◇ Hire date
  ◇ Full-time, part-time, or temporary status
  ◇ Compensation
  ◇ Organizational chart
◆ Biographies/resumes of key employees
  ◇ Structure of key employee compensation
◆ Agreements related to employment, independent contractors, consultants, directors, or officers, including information on commissions, severance, and change in control agreements
◆ Confidentiality, noncompete, commission, and trade secret agreements (present and former employees, consultants, or other third parties)

- All agreements, contracts, or commitments limiting the ability of the company to engage in any line of business, compete with any other person, or solicit any person for employment with the company
- Employee handbooks, manuals, personnel policy manuals, and policies not part of any manual
- Employee work rules
- Union or collective bargaining agreements:
  - ◇ Covering any group or unit of employees
  - ◇ National Labor Relations Board (NLRB) certifications that may trigger potential successorship obligations or liabilities
  - ◇ Expired, pending, scheduled, or expected to be scheduled
  - ◇ Internal grievance procedures and on-solicitation and no-access rules related to union issues
- Description of any labor law violations, "Prohibited Transactions" (as defined by Section 4975 of IRS Code or Section 406 of Employee Retirement Income Security Act) as well as any "accumulated funding deficiencies" (as defined by ERISA)
- Subcontractor labor agreements
- Samples of all application forms
- EEO-1 (Employer Information Report), if applicable, for past three years
- Any document prepared by the company or at the company's request that might be subject to discovery in future discrimination cases
- All documents related to I-9 compliance, including any letters (in the past two years) from the Social Security Administration regarding employees' social security numbers
- Copies of any notices prepared or served related to Workers Adjustment and Retraining Notification Act (WARN)
- Compliance with federal and state withholding requirements
- Copies of any affirmative action plan adopted pursuant to federal, state, or local statute, rule, or regulation, including, but not limited to, Executive Order 11246 and its implementing regulations
- Copies of all correspondence, documentation, annual reports (if applicable), summary plan descriptions, determination letters, and actuarial reports (for the past five years) for any and all:
  - ◇ Group insurance plans
  - ◇ Pension and profit-sharing plans (or any plan described in Section 3 of the Employee Retirement Income Security Act of 1974)

◇   Bonus and incentive compensation plans:
  ○   Stock option plans (restricted or unrestricted)
  ○   Stock appreciation rights plans
  ○   Nonqualified deferred compensation plans
  ○   Performance share or other awards
  ○   Welfare and fringe benefit plans
  ○   Voluntary employees' beneficiary association (VEBA) trust agreements
◇   Deferred compensation and salary continuation plans
◇   Bonus plans or arrangements
◇   Incentive compensation plans and phantom stock plans
◇   Severance agreements
- List of employees receiving COBRA benefits
- List of employees' current vacation and sick leave accruals
- List of leaves of absence (requested or granted) within the last 180 days, including reasons for request and/or permission for leave
- List of employees receiving short-term or long-term disability payments
- List of all employees on layoff
- List of pending garnishment and wage assignment obligations
- List of policies regarding employee loans and any outstanding employee loans from, and debts to, the company
- Any documents that refer to or create rights by employees to severance payments
- List of other employee benefits not covered above

8. Insurance

- Schedules/certificates/binders related to:
  ◇   Health
  ◇   Vehicles
  ◇   Property
  ◇   Product liability
  ◇   Casualty
  ◇   Business interruption and discontinuance
  ◇   Key person
  ◇   Directors/officers fiduciary liability
  ◇   Personal injury
  ◇   Workers' compensation

- Copies of any summaries of insurance coverage
- List of pending uninsured claims
- Outstanding workers' compensation claims
- Insurance claims (of any type) during past five years
- Notification of termination of coverage from insurers during past five years
- Documents related to payment of contributions, interest, or penalties for unemployment insurance within past five years
- List of any other insurance-related documents not covered above

9. Litigation

- List of all pending or threatened lawsuits, claims, grievances (asserted and nonasserted), and assessments (within the past five years) noting:
    ◇ Whether claim has been resolved
    ◇ Whether subject to an award
    ◇ Whether insurer has accepted liability (if applicable)
    ◇ Nature of proceedings
    ◇ Date of commencement
    ◇ Current status
    ◇ Relief sought
    ◇ Estimated and/or actual costs
- Settlement agreements, conciliation agreements, releases, and state, territorial, or federal court or agency orders in injunctions involving any incumbent or former company employees entered into or issued within the past five years
- Potential claims
- Administrative proceedings
- Actions or proceedings (past, pending, or threatened) before state, territorial, and federal courts or agencies involving labor, employment, safety, and employee benefit matters, including:
    ◇ Employment discrimination charges
    ◇ Wage and hour investigation and complaints
    ◇ Occupational Safety and Health Administration (OSHA) investigations and complaints

◇ Office of Federal Contract Compliance Programs (OFCCP) investigations and complaints

◇ Employment tax audits

◇ Immigration and Naturalization Service audits

◇ Charges of retaliation under antidiscrimination or workers' compensation laws

◇ Grievances under collective bargaining agreements

◇ Unfair labor practice charges

◇ Representation proceedings

◇ Audits or claims by trust funds providing pension and health insurance to bargaining unit employees

◇ Union organizing activity

◆ Copies of any correspondence or other documentation involving the return of merchandise based on a claim that such merchandise was defective

◆ Copies of all consent decrees, judgments, other decrees, orders, and settlement agreements to which the company, or any of its officers, directors, nominees for director, key employees, or controlling stockholders is a party or is bound that relate to environmental, health, and safety (EHS) matters or liabilities of the company

◆ Copies of all documents related to all civil, criminal, or administrative claims, lawsuits, or actions (threatened, pending, or resolved) under EHS laws or concerning EHS matters to which the company is or was a party, or is or was otherwise involved, including:

◇ All material agreements under which the company is obligated to take any action or make any payment for environmental cleanup or compliance or under which the company is obligated to indemnify any other party for investigation, assessment, testing, removal, or remediation of hazardous substances (for purposes here referred to as "hazardous substances" to be broadly defined and to include petroleum)

◆ Copies of letters from attorneys for the company to the company's independent public accountants concerning litigation and other legal proceedings related to EHS laws (i.e., "audit letters")

◆ List of any litigation-related issues not covered above

10. Permits, Registrations, Licenses, Authorizations, Certificates, Concessions, and Registrations Related to Government Compliance (Referred to Collectively as "Permits")

Concerning the conduct of the company's business required by federal, state, or local governmental agencies, bureaus, or boards:

◆ List and copies of all
◆ List of jurisdictions outside home state where the company has facilities or authority to transact business
◆ List and copies of documents requesting renewal of any permits expiring in current year
◆ Discussion of compliance with applicable government regulations or standards related to:
  ◇ Safety of products
  ◇ Safety in company facilities (OSHA)
    ○ Include list/description of hazardous work conditions or known or suspected violations of OSHA requirements and hazardous waste disposal
  ◇ Equal employment opportunity
  ◇ Wages and hours
  ◇ U.S. Environmental Protection Agency (EPA)
  ◇ U.S. Food and Drug Administration (FDA)
  ◇ U.S. Department of Transportation
  ◇ U.S. Department of Homeland Security
  ◇ Pricing, sale, and distribution of products
  ◇ Import/export permits/licenses
  ◇ Violations cited in inspections in last twelve months
◆ Copies of all contracts with any governmental agencies that require compliance with state, territorial, or federal prevailing wage laws or affirmative action programs for applications, employees, or enterprises owned by minorities or women
◆ Any information concerning required security clearances to business with certain entities
◆ Copies of any industrial revenue bonds and other government-sponsored loans and all material documents related thereto
◆ Copies of all documents, correspondence, and filings relating to governmental/regulatory agency claims, assessments, and proceedings (pending or threatened)

- Copies of all correspondence during the past five years with the U.S. Department of Justice, the Federal Trade Commission, the U.S. Environmental Protection Agency, or any other governmental, administrative, or regulatory agency, whether state or federal
- Copies of all inspection or other reports issued by administrative or regulatory agencies
- Copies of any report, internal compliance audit, regulatory review, or other investigation by the company (or any other party) related to the company's compliance with any law, regulation, ordinance, rule, or code

11. Environment Related

- List and copies of environmental, health, and safety (EHS) permits
  ◇ Current
  ◇ Expired
  ◇ Yet to be obtained
- Records of any hazardous substance spills or releases from any site currently or formerly owned or leased by the company
- Copies of any communication from any source related to the Comprehensive Environmental Response, Compensation, and Liability Act (CERCLA) or any EHS law
- List of names and addresses of all past and current off-site waste disposal facilities and transporters used by the company
  ◇ Include sites used for recycling or reclamation
  ◇ Describe the waste sent to each site
  ◇ Note the time period in which the company sent waste to each site
- Description of the company's EHS compliance program
  ◇ Copies of documents related to any programs designed to comply with process safety management or reduce management risk
  ◇ Documents related to compliance with Department of Homeland Security regulations
- Copies of all documents related to any indemnification the company has given or received involving liability for EHS matters, along with documents related to any claims made or received

- Copies of all documents related to environmental issues
  - ◇ Include audits, studies, environmental sampling data, reports, site evaluations, government filings, agreements, consent decrees, consent orders, all Phase I and Phase II environmental assessments, and Phase III and any remedial action reports
  - ◇ Include those applicable to the company, its predecessors, and its affiliates
  - ◇ Include those related to current or prior facilities (whether owned or leased)
  - ◇ Include any soil or groundwater sampling conducted at any real property owned or leased by the company
- Copies of air emission inventories:
  - ◇ Include for each facility owned or leased by the company
  - ◇ Document actual emissions for past five years
  - ◇ Include any analysis or review of the applicability of greenhouse gas reporting rule to the company's emissions
- All information related to generation, treatment, disposal, or recycling of hazardous substances and/or solid wastes
  - ◇ Include history of problems or other issues with pollution control and environmental contamination
  - ◇ Include any communications with federal or state environmental agencies
- List of all dangerous, toxic, flammable, or hazardous substances used, produced, or disposed of in connection with the operations or business of the company
  - ◇ Indicate whether a company's current or prior facilities were used
- List of all storage tanks currently (or previously) owned, leased, or operated either by the company or on any real property currently or previously owned or leased by the company, indicating (for each tank):
  - ◇ The nature of materials stored in the tank
  - ◇ Copies of documents related to registration, releases, monitoring, testing, and closure
- Information related to any nuisance complaints (e.g., odor, noise, migration of contamination) received by the company under any EHS law or regulation or under common law
- Documents related to energy efficiency, or reduction programs or measures taken by the company in the past five years

- Documents submitted to governmental authority or prepared pursuant to any community or worker right-to-know law (program, law, or requirement) similar to the Emergency Planning and Community Right-to-Know Act
- List of any environment-related documents not covered above

12. Accounts

- List of ten largest customers
  - ◇ Sales to each for the past three years
- List of suppliers (by dollar volume) and related contracts (for past three fiscal years and year-to-date)
- All vendor contracts
- Examples of all standard form agreements (short-term leases, purchase or sale orders, invoices, requisitions, service contracts, etc.) used by the company with suppliers or customers, along with a list of all existing contracts or leases in each form that have not otherwise been provided

13. Accounts Receivable

- Detailed accounts receivable aging and reconciliation to general ledger (most recent month-end that ties to balance sheet)
- Analysis of bad debt expense and write-offs for the past three years
- Explanation of credit issues
- Schedule of notes and loans receivable

14. Prepaid Accounts

- Schedule of prepaid expenses

15. Inventory

- List of inventory by department, item, and reconciliation to general ledger
- Analysis of inventory write-offs, obsolescence, and write-downs (past three years)

◆ Inventory breakdown by category, turns, and aging
  ◇ Identify any inventory that is unique or custom or has a very specific application
  ◇ Identify any consigned inventory (held at customer's location)
◆ Written description of all policies/procedures relating to inventory and returned product

16. Fixed Assets

(Includes machinery; equipment; tooling; office furniture, fixtures, and inventory; and leasehold improvements)
  ◆ List of material, machinery, equipment, or inventory
    ◇ Note whether in possession of company or third party
    ◇ Note dates of acquisition
    ◇ Note whether subject to lien, encumbrance, or security interest.
    ◇ Include copies of Uniform Commercial Code (UCC) search reports as applicable
  ◆ Copies of all:
    ◇ Bills of sale
    ◇ Leases (equipment and motor vehicle)
    ◇ Financing agreements
    ◇ Security agreements
    ◇ Applicable insurance
  ◆ Copies of all contracts or options to purchase, sell, or lease personal property
  ◆ Copies of all installment contracts for the purchase of personal property, including equipment
  ◆ Detailed schedule and reconciliation to general ledger

17. Real Property

  ◆ Owned:
    ◇ List of all real property owned in fee and locations thereof (and any related mortgages, indentures/promissory notes, and trust deeds)
    ◇ Fixture filings with respect to real property
    ◇ Copies of contract and options to purchase or sell real property or to construct improvements thereon

◆ Leased:
   ◇ List of all leases and subleases on any locations/facilities utilized by the company or its employees or on which it pays taxes on a recurring basis, including square footage
   ◇ Copies of any assignments of lease made for security purposes or otherwise
◆ Leased or owned:
   ◇ List of all liens or encumbrances against real property
   ◇ Copies of any appraisals of real property
   ◇ Copies of any surveys relating to real property
   ◇ Copies of any engineering reports prepared regarding real property
   ◇ Copies of certificates of occupancy
   ◇ Copies of any governmental permits required with respect to real property
   ◇ Copies of any guarantees or warranties relating to improvements on real property
   ◇ Copies of any outstanding notices of violation or similar notices received from any governmental authority or insurance company related to the use, operation, or maintenance of real property
   ◇ List of condemnation or eminent domain proceedings pending or threatened against real property
   ◇ List of those properties (owned, leased, or operated currently or previously) for which the company has retained or assumed environmental liabilities, description of the type of operations conducted at each property, and dates of ownership, tenancy, or operation
◆ Owned in the past:
   ◇ List of any real property formerly owned or leased by the company since its date of incorporation
   ◇ Copies of all prior title insurance policies and title reports and/or opinions, including copies of exceptions listed on said policies
◆ Future plans:
   ◇ Description of any plans the company has with respect to opening or closing of any operating facility

18. Intellectual Property

- For all patents, trademarks, service marks, copyrights, trade names, domain names, and other industrial property rights:
  - ◇ Copies of all registrations, assignments, and licenses (including dates registrations were filed)
  - ◇ Copies of all pending applications, including where and when such applications were filed
  - ◇ List indicating which are unregistered or common-law
  - ◇ List indicating which are owned by third parties, licensed to the company, or used in connection with the business of the company (with copies of all related agreements)
- Licensing agreements, contracts, options, or agreements that relate in any manner to intellectual property
- Detailed list of all computer systems
  - ◇ Leases and licenses
- Infringement actions
  - ◇ Disclose if the company has received any notice, claim, or threat that:
    1. Company does not own any intellectual property it claims to own
    2. Company does not have the right to use any intellectual property that it claims to license from a third party
    3. Any intellectual property owned by or licensed to company is invalid or unenforceable
  - ◇ Provide copies of such notices or claims, a complete description of said notice or claim, copies of all correspondence related to the claim/notice, the circumstances surrounding it, any responsive actions taken by the company, and the current status of said notice or claim
- Trade secrets
  - ◇ List and describe all material trade secrets owned by or licensed to the company
  - ◇ Include copies of representative employment agreements, independent contractor agreements, and company policies related to the protection of trade secrets or ownership of intellectual property
  - ◇ Provide copies of all assignments, licenses, and nondisclosure and other agreements related to trade secrets

- ◇ List all third parties to which the company has disclosed any of its trade secrets and provide copies of the agreements that control these disclosures; if no agreements were used, please provide explanation
- ◇ If the company has obtained trade secrets for confidential information from a third party, describe the steps the company takes to ensure that it uses such trade secrets (or confidential information) only in the manner in which it is authorized to do so
- ◇ Provide copies of all materials related to any charges of trade secret misappropriation made by, on behalf of, or against the company
- ◆ List products that the company has reverse-engineered and provide all agreements relating to such products. For each such product, indicate whether:
  1. The company manufactured the product pursuant to a formula provided by a customer
  2. To the company's knowledge, the product is subject to any patents

19. Marketing and Sales Materials
- ◆ Agreements with advertising/public relations agencies
- ◆ All marketing or sales materials
- ◆ Certifications or preferred status designations, customer awards, etc.
- ◆ Copy of any press release related to the company within the past five years
- ◆ Copies of all advertising and labeling agreements

20. Research and Development
- ◆ Contracts

21. Transaction Intermediary and Finders' Fees
- ◆ Contracts
- ◆ List of any nonwritten agreements

Management System
Due Diligence List

Item	Presale DD	Buyer DD
I. Customer and Product Performance		
A. Revenues, gross margin, and units for all customers for past five years.	X* – Top 10 customers for past three years. – Note percentage of sales.	X
1. Segmented by end-market application		X
B. Name of each customer:		X
1. Length of relationship		
C. Schedule of historical price increases by:	X Indicate most recent price increase.	X
1. Customer		
2. Amount		
3. Timing		

Item	Presale DD	Buyer DD
D. Explanation for any and all lost customers (past five years).	X – Three years – Major customers (not any and all).	X
E. Details of any material customer contracts.	X Indicate whether a change in ownership affects these contracts.	X
II. Production and Supply Chain Analysis		

A. Schedule of costs for each raw material component (past four years).
 	
   1. Annual purchase volumes and associated prices organized by:
     a. Specification
     b. Price per pound
     c. Supplier for the primary raw materials used in the manufacture of the product
	X
	Indicate whether company is dependent on any vendors.
		X

B. Provide any material supplier contacts and key terms.	X Indicate if a change in ownership affects these contracts.	X
C. Provide details on rebate programs with suppliers.	X Explain any rebate programs that skew financials.	X
D. Estimate the equipment costs necessary to start manufacturing in-house those products that are currently outsourced.		X
E. Provide labor and overhead detail related to manufacturing for past four years:	X – Three years	X
1. Labor and overhead cost per unit		X
2. Number of production overtime hours		X
3. Number of units run by product line	X	X
4. Number of lines in plant	X	X
5. Run speeds, setup time, changeover time on current lines	X	X
F. Provide order information as follows:		
1. Number shipped daily	X	X
2. Number of trucks shipped daily		X
3. Average size of truckload	X	X
4. Average shipping cost per unit	X	X

Item	Presale DD	Buyer DD
G. For manufacturing employees (excluding plan supervisor), list:		
1. Average wage rate	X	X
2. Starting wage rate	X	X
H. For each operating line identify:		
1. Payroll complete with title and salary		X
2. Volume of production by unit size		X
I. List any special packaging requirements for company's products:	Are there any special packaging requirements?	X
1. Labels, shrink packaging, etc.		X
J. Describe any customer-specific requirements.	Are there any customer-specific requirements?	X
K. Describe any stock-level programs.	X	X
L. Provide a company organizational chart organized by functional area.	X	X
M. Provide payroll information by:		
1. Department		X
2. Title		X
3. Salary		X
N. Provide sales coverage map by geographic area:		
1. Include associated marketing collateral.	X	X
2. Include foreign countries to which company exports.	X	X
O. Provide sales coverage map by salesperson:		
1. Include associated marketing collateral.		X
2. Include foreign countries to which company exports.		X
III. Technical Product Analysis		
A. Provide access to all formulas and labels.		X
B. Describe any pending litigation related to product safety or other regulatory matters.	X	X
C. Describe legal compliance efforts related to all applicable regulations (e.g., EPA and OSHA).	Is company in compliance with all regulatory requirements?	X

Item	Presale DD	Buyer DD
D. Provide access to all raw material, Material Safety Data Sheets, and tools for MSDS authoring.		X
E. Provide details on mechanisms for change management/control.		X
F. Describe customer complaint processing and related call history.		X
G. Provide details related to any major product liability claim in the past five years.	Have you experienced any claims related to insurance or liability?	X
H. Provide detailed information on regulatory/ EPA permits, registrations, etc.	Is company in compliance with all regulatory requirements?	X
I. Provide name and version of all manufacturing software.	X	X
IV. Customer/Market Review		
A. Provide any relevant customer or market surveys conducted in the past five years.	X for three years	X
V. Insurance Review		
A. Provide complete copies of all current policies.		X
B. For each policy include:		X
1. Currently valued loss run (for the past five years) 2. Complete history		X X
C. Complete copies of any contracts and/or licenses requiring special insurance wording.		X
VI. Environmental Review		
A. Provide copies of any environmental reports.		X
B. Provide copies of any sampling results.		X
C. Describe status of any known environmental conditions.	Does company have any environmental issues?	X

Checking an Investment Banker's References

These questions are designed for owners/prospective sellers to ask former owners who retained the investment banker they are considering for their own transaction.

1. When did you close on the sale of your business?

2. How long did the sale process take from the time you signed the investment banker's engagement letter until closing?

3. Did you get the purchase price you wanted?

4. Do you think that the investment banker really understood your company and your goals?

5. How did the investment banker market your company?

6. Did the investment banker protect your confidentiality throughout the process?

7. Did the investment banker keep you abreast of every important development?

8. How would you rate this investment banker's:
   a. Judgment?
   b. Negotiating skills?
   c. Ability to predict problems and solve them?

9. Did you feel prepared when you eventually met the buyer?

10. Was this investment banker available when you needed him or her?

11. If you had to sell another company, would you use the same investment banker?

What to Look for in an Engagement Letter

Selling your company is a huge undertaking: financially, emotionally, legally, and personally. Like all transactions in which you retain an individual or a firm to represent you, that relationship is governed by a contractual agreement, usually in the form of an engagement letter. I suggest that you ask your attorney to review any engagement letter that you consider signing to make sure that it satisfies the legal requirements in your state and that it protects your interest.

1. Services

What services does the investment bank say it will perform?

- ◆ Will it use an existing list of possible buyers or develop a unique list for your company based on its access to a number of databases?
- ◆ Will it charge for meetings with your accountant and lawyer, or are those meetings included in its fee?

- Who pays for the establishment and maintenance of the virtual data room? This online site is maintained by a third party and contains all of your company's information (financial statements, employment and all other contracts, leases, invoices, written policies, etc.) for review by potential buyers. Security is critical, as are protocols regarding password access to increasingly sensitive materials.
- Does the investment bank commit to communicating with you:
    ◇ Verbally or in writing?
    ◇ On a prearranged basis or as necessary?
- What services will the investment bank not perform? Excluded services can include providing tax, legal, or accounting advice. Some investment banks perform due diligence; others do not.
- Who in the investment bank will negotiate the transaction? The same person you meet initially? A junior person?

2. Fees

Investment banks typically charge a retainer as well as a contingent fee.

- *Retainer fee.* Investment bankers charge a retainer fee to commit a seller to the sale process. Investment bankers don't want to invest time and money into bringing a company to market, only to have the seller change his or her mind.
    ◇ When is the retainer fee due?
    ◇ Can it be paid in installments?

- *Contingent fee.* This fee typically represents the lion's share of the amount you'll pay an investment banker because it is typically a percentage of the purchase price. In customizing the banker's fee, first come to an agreement about your minimally acceptable sale price. The banker's fee for achieving that sale price should be minimal, say, 2.5 percent. From that point, increase the percentage on amounts over that price to motivate the investment banker to negotiate aggressively on your behalf.

Most firms establish a minimum fee (due at closing and unrelated to the purchase price). From there, investment bankers may set percentages due on portions of the purchase price.

For example, the fee might be:

- 2.5 percent of the minimally acceptable sale price (say, $10 million)
- 3.5 percent of the purchase price between $10,000,001 and $15,000,000
- 5 percent of the purchase price between $15,000,001 and $20,000,000
- 6 percent of the purchase price above $20,000,000

You'll note that the percentages increase as the purchase price increases. The purpose here is to encourage your investment banker to work for the best possible price.

There are other contingent fee formulas, one of which (known as the *Lehman formula*) reduces the investment banker's percentage as the purchase price rises. Think carefully about how you wish to motivate the investment banker working on your behalf.

3. Purchase Price

Generally, the purchase price includes far more than the cash that changes hands at closing. It is impossible to list all the issues the definition of *purchase price* might include because of the fluidity and variability in the design of each transaction. In general, however, you can expect the purchase price to include:

- The value of any stock, debt, or other financial instruments (including warrants and stock options) issued in consideration, plus
- The total of any liabilities assumed, including any debt, trade payables, and other liabilities on the balance sheet, and any contingent or other liabilities that may not be on the company's balance sheet, plus
- The value of any assets (cash, accounts receivable, inventory, real estate, etc.) retained by the sellers (company or shareholders), plus
- The value of any stock retained by the sellers (company or shareholders), plus
- The present value, at the then-current prime rate, of any employment or noncompete contracts, rents, royalties, and any other forms of deferred payment related to the compensation of the transaction

If your employment agreement remains the same after closing as it was before closing, the investment banker is not likely to take a cut. He or she should be paid only if a significant portion of the purchase price is paid to you via your postsale employment contract.

❖

A note of explanation about charging a fee on stock retained by the seller: Your investment banker may be able to negotiate a deal in which the purchaser agrees to buy only a portion of your stock. The investment banker wants his or her fee paid as if 100 percent of the stock were transferred because you have benefited—thanks to the investment banker's negotiating prowess—from selling the majority of your company while retaining an interest in its future prosperity.

❖ ❖

4. Expenses

Some engagement letters list the charges for various expenses (travel, courier charges, and copy charges). Others set an amount that, if exceeded, you must preapprove.

5. Exclusivity

All investment banks require you to contractually agree that they will act as your exclusive representative. Exclusivity also means that if a potential buyer contacts you after you sign the engagement letter, you will use your investment banker to represent you in negotiations with that prospective buyer. Some sellers want to "carve out" a specific buyer. Before you ask your investment banker to do so, remember that the competitive auction process (the sale process most likely to yield a maximum sale price) works best when all buyers compete to purchase your company. If you exclude one buyer from that process, it is likely to offer far less for your company than it would if included in the competitive auction process. Don't be surprised if investment bankers refuse to represent you if you tie their hands by removing a legitimate buyer from the sale process.

6. Termination

Sellers do well to pay close attention to this part of the engagement letter. It should clearly state how each party can terminate the contract, and when. Most important, it states that the seller is obligated to pay the banker's fee—if that seller sells to: (a) any buyer or (b) any buyer contacted by the investment banker—and for how long that obligation to pay is in force. For example, some investment bankers want a one-year "tail" after the termination, and others may want five years. You obviously want to negotiate for the shortest period of time and should stipulate that the investment banker must provide you a list (upon termination) of all prospective buyers contacted. You may wish to negotiate the requirements for being placed on that list. For example, perhaps it includes only those prospective buyers that signed a nondisclosure agreement.

7. Legal Stuff

This section includes naming the state whose laws will govern the agreement. It is usually the state where the investment bank is headquartered, but this can be negotiated.

It also includes "hold harmless" clauses whereby you agree that the investment banker will depend on the accuracy of the material you provide and that you'll seek your own accounting and legal advice. You will also likely be asked to hold harmless the investment bank (and everyone related to it) if you are (or it is) sued or damaged, in any way, by the transaction. Make sure that you are not responsible for any liabilities arising from the negligence, bad faith, or willful misconduct of your investment bank. Make sure that you are as well protected from the actions of the investment bank as it is protected from yours.

Finally, expect some sort of arbitration clause that puts all disputes that can't be worked within a reasonable amount of time (say, thirty days) into arbitration. Make sure you have the same rights to submit a dispute to arbitration as the investment bank has.

Sample Nondisclosure Agreement

Between
Owner as Protected Party and Investment Banker as Receiving Party
or
Investment Banker as Protected Party and Prospective Buyer as Receiving
Party

This Agreement is made between _____ authorized represen-

tative of _____ (hereinafter referred to as the "Protected Party")

and _____ authorized representative for _____

(hereinafter referred to as "Receiving Party").

A. RECEIVING PARTY AGREES TO THE FOLLOWING:

1. It will actively protect the confidentiality of all information, data, and materials disclosed or furnished in writing or orally (herein called "Information") by the Protected Party.

2. In consideration for such disclosure, Receiving Party and its employees will use the Information only for internal evaluation purposes.

3. It understands that any disclosure of any of the Information (including the possibility that the Shareholders may consider sale), disclosure of the current status of the Protected Party, or disclosure of any Information to customers, vendors, competitors, or employees of the Protected Party would cause serious financial damage to the Protected Party and/or its affiliates.

4. It will not, for the term of this Agreement, solicit for employment any person who is currently employed by the Protected Party.

5. It will not copy, duplicate, disclose, or deliver all or any portion of the Information to a third party or permit any third party to inspect, copy, or duplicate the same.

B. NOTHING STATED ABOVE SHALL PREVENT THE RECEIVING PARTY FROM DISCLOSING TO OTHERS OR USING IN ANY MANNER:

1. Information that has been published and has become part of the public domain other than by acts or omissions by the Receiving Party.

2. Information that has been furnished or made known to the Receiving Party by third parties as a matter of right without restriction of disclosure.

3. Information that the Receiving Party can show was already in its possession at the time it entered into this Agreement and which was not acquired directly or indirectly from the Company, its representatives, its employees, or their representatives.

C. THIS AGREEMENT SHALL REMAIN IN EFFECT FOR A TERM OF TWO YEARS FROM THE EXECUTION DATE HEREOF, AND, UPON REQUEST, THE RECEIVING PARTY WILL PROMPTLY RETURN ALL DATA AND MATERIALS FURNISHED BY THE PROTECTED PARTY AND DESTROY ANY INTERNAL ANALYSES AND/OR WORK PAPERS RELATED TO THE PROTECTED PARTY.

Signature: _____

For Protected Party: _____

Signature: _____

For Receiving Party: _____

Questions to Ask a Prospective Investment Banker

1. Can he or she provide a valuation that takes into account:
   a. Current market conditions in your industry?
   b. Future performance of your company?
   c. Understanding of buyers in the marketplace?
   d. Unique characteristics of your company?
   e. Terms a buyer is likely to demand?

2. Does he or she understand what makes your company unique?

3. Does he or she have enough experience to anticipate future challenges and develop successful strategies to overcome those challenges?

4. Does he or she have the analytical skills necessary to understand your company's numbers and the ability to persuade the buyer to see them as he or she does?

5. Does he or she have the reputation in the professional community necessary to recruit other members to your advisory team?

6. Does he or she understand the world of buyers well enough to find the right buyer for your company?

7. Can he or she develop creative market strategies to successfully orchestrate a competitive auction and get an Outrageous Price for your company?

8. Does he or she have enough experience and the good judgment to help you prioritize buyers?

9. Is his or her reputation in the marketplace one that facilitates introductions to decision makers? Does this reputation reflect well on you?

10. Can he or she tell a compelling story? Can he or she communicate clearly and effectively?

11. Does he or she know how to attract buyers to the table?

12. Is he or she as sensitive about confidentiality as you are?

13. Does he or she recognize the fine line between "just enough" and "too much" information?

14. Can he or she recognize the difference between serious and half-hearted buyers?

15. Does he or she understand your needs well enough to find the buyer that "fits" you?

16. Can he or she script a site visit that prepares you for the unexpected?

17. Can he or she orchestrate site visits in a way that makes you comfortable?

18. Does he or she know how to maintain deal momentum?

19. Does he or she know how to control the flow of information?

20. Does he or she know how to elicit positive indications of terms and value from buyers?

21. Can he or she evaluate deal structures in terms of your goals?

22. Does he or she know where the buyer has hidden "land mines" (in the letter of intent and purchase agreement) that have the potential to reduce the purchase price *after* closing?

23. Can he or she efficiently organize all of your company's information to minimize the time and effort necessary to complete due diligence?

24. Can he or she manage the release of company information so that it supports the company's projection of future growth?

25. Can he or she manage the due diligence process so that precious time is not wasted?

26. Can he or she track all the open issues quickly and efficiently enough to maintain deal momentum?

27. Does he or she have the experience necessary to distinguish the important from the trivial while negotiating the promises you'll make in your warranties and representations?

28. Does he or she have the attention to detail necessary to collect (from a myriad of sources) every single deliverable necessary to close the deal?

29. Does he or she understand the nuances of negotiation? Can he or she help you understand your options and make decisions?

30. Will he or she be there *whenever* you need him or her?

References

Baumeister, Roy F., and John Tierney. *Willpower: Rediscovering the Greatest Human Strength.* New York: Penguin Press, 2011.

Porter, Michael E. *Competitive Advantage: Creating and Sustaining Superior Performance.* New York: Free Press, 1985.

Porter, Michael E. *Competitive Strategy: Techniques for Analyzing Industries and Competitors.* New York: Free Press, 1980, new introduction 1998.

Subramanian, Guhan. *Negotiauctions: New Dealmaking Strategies for a Competitive Marketplace.* New York: W. W. Norton & Company, 2010.

Index